LEARN AAVE DEFI PROTOCOL

100+ Coding Q&A

Yasin Cakal

Code of Code

CONTENTS

Title Page

Copyright

Introduction

Overview of AAVE Protocol   1

How AAVE Protocol Differs from other DeFi Protocols   4

Installing Dependencies and Tools   7

Setting Up a Local AAVE Test Environment   11

Overview of the AAVE Protocol Architecture   15

Key Components of the AAVE Protocol   19

Understanding the Different Types of Smart Contracts in AAVE Protocol   23

Interacting with AAVE Smart Contracts Using Web3   27

Understanding the Lending and Borrowing Process on AAVE   31

Implementing Lending and Borrowing Functionality in your Code   35

Understanding Liquidation and Collateral in AAVE   40

Implementing Liquidation and Collateral Functionality in your Code   44

Overview of AAVE Protocol Governance   54

Implementing Staking Functionality in Your Code   57

Implementing Flash Loans in our Code   63

Utilizing AAVE Protocol for Stablecoin Lending and Borrowing   67

Integrating AAVE Protocol with other DeFi Protocols   72

Recap of Key Concepts Learned in the Course   81

Further Resources and Tips for Staying Up to Date   84

Thank You   87

INTRODUCTION

Welcome to "Learn AAVE DeFi Protocol", the comprehensive book designed to help blockchain developers master the AAVE protocol and create innovative decentralized finance (DeFi) applications. If you're looking to expand your blockchain development skills and join the growing DeFi ecosystem, this book is for you.

In this book, you'll be guided through every aspect of working with AAVE protocol, from setting up your development environment to implementing advanced features such as flash loans and stablecoin lending and borrowing. You'll also learn about the key components of the AAVE protocol, such as smart contracts, lending and borrowing, liquidation and collateral, and governance and staking.

Throughout the book, you'll have the opportunity to apply your knowledge through hands-on coding exercises and examples, ensuring that you have a solid understanding of the material. By the end of the book, you'll be able to confidently build DeFi applications using AAVE protocol and join the ranks of skilled blockchain developers in the DeFi space.

So if you're ready to take your blockchain development skills to the next level and enter the exciting world of DeFi, join us now for "Learn AAVE DeFi Protocol"!

OVERVIEW OF AAVE PROTOCOL

AAVE protocol is a decentralized finance (DeFi) platform that allows users to lend and borrow a variety of assets in a transparent and secure manner. Built on the Ethereum blockchain, AAVE protocol utilizes smart contracts and a decentralized governance model to facilitate open and permissionless access to financial services. In this article, we'll provide a comprehensive overview of AAVE protocol, including its key features, benefits, and use cases.

What is AAVE Protocol?

AAVE protocol is a decentralized lending and borrowing platform that allows users to earn interest on their idle assets and borrow assets they need, all without the need for a traditional financial institution. By using smart contracts to automate the process of lending and borrowing, AAVE protocol allows users to access financial services in a fast, secure, and transparent manner.

One of the key features of AAVE protocol is its use of a decentralized governance model, which allows the AAVE community to collectively decide on important protocol updates and changes. This model ensures that AAVE protocol remains open and permissionless, allowing anyone to access and use the platform.

Key Features of AAVE Protocol

AAVE protocol offers a wide range of features that make it a powerful tool for decentralized finance. Some of the key features of AAVE protocol include:

- Lending and borrowing: AAVE protocol allows users to lend and borrow a variety of assets, including cryptocurrencies such as Bitcoin and Ethereum, as well as stablecoins like DAI and USDC. Users can earn interest on their idle assets by lending them out, or borrow assets they need by using their existing assets as collateral.
- Liquidation and collateral: To ensure the security of the AAVE platform, AAVE protocol uses a system of liquidation and collateral to protect lenders in the event that a borrower defaults on their loan. If a borrower's collateral falls below a certain value, the AAVE protocol will automatically sell off the collateral to pay back the loan, minimizing losses for the lender.
- Governance and staking: As mentioned previously, AAVE protocol uses a decentralized governance model to allow the community to collectively decide on important protocol updates and changes. Users can participate in governance by staking their AAVE tokens, which gives them voting rights and the ability to propose and vote on governance proposals.

Benefits of Using AAVE Protocol

AAVE protocol offers a number of benefits for users, including:

- Fast and secure transactions: By using smart contracts and the Ethereum blockchain, AAVE protocol allows for fast and secure transactions that are automatically executed and recorded on the blockchain.
- Transparent and open access: AAVE protocol is open and permissionless, meaning anyone can access and use the platform. In addition, the use of smart contracts ensures that all transactions are transparent and can be easily verified on the blockchain.
- Decentralized governance: The decentralized governance model of AAVE protocol allows the community to collectively decide on important updates and changes, ensuring that the platform remains open and permissionless.

Use Cases for AAVE Protocol

AAVE protocol has a number of potential use cases, including:

- Cryptocurrency lending and borrowing: AAVE protocol allows users to lend and borrow a variety of cryptocurrencies, including Bitcoin and Ethereum. This can be useful for traders looking to earn interest on their idle assets or for those who need to borrow assets for short-term trading purposes.
- Stablecoin lending and borrowing: AAVE protocol also supports lending and borrowing of stablecoins such as DAI and USDC. This can be useful for users who want to earn interest on their stablecoins or for those who need to borrow stablecoins for various purposes.
- Decentralized borrowing and lending platform: AAVE protocol can be used as a decentralized platform for borrowing and lending a variety of assets, including traditional fiat currencies and commodities. This allows users to access financial services without the need for a traditional financial institution.
- DeFi liquidity provision: AAVE protocol can be used by liquidity providers to earn interest on their idle assets by providing liquidity to DeFi protocols. This can help to drive adoption and growth of the DeFi ecosystem.
- DeFi insurance: AAVE protocol can be used to create decentralized insurance products that protect against losses in the DeFi ecosystem. This can help to increase trust and confidence in DeFi protocols.

Conclusion

AAVE protocol is a decentralized lending and borrowing platform that allows users to access financial services in a fast, secure, and transparent manner. With its wide range of features and potential use cases, AAVE protocol is poised to play a key role in the growing DeFi ecosystem. Whether you're a lender looking to earn interest on your idle assets, a borrower in need of short-term financing, or a developer looking to build DeFi applications, AAVE protocol has something to offer.

Exercises

To review these concepts, we will go through a series of exercises designed to test your understanding and apply what you have learned.

What is AAVE protocol?
What are some key features of AAVE protocol?
What are some benefits of using AAVE protocol?

What are some potential use cases for AAVE protocol?
How does AAVE protocol differ from traditional financial institutions?

Solutions

What is AAVE protocol?

AAVE protocol is a decentralized lending and borrowing platform that allows users to earn interest on their idle assets and borrow assets they need, all without the need for a traditional financial institution.

What are some key features of AAVE protocol?

Some key features of AAVE protocol include lending and borrowing, liquidation and collateral, and governance and staking.

What are some benefits of using AAVE protocol?

Some benefits of using AAVE protocol include fast and secure transactions, transparent and open access, and decentralized governance.

What are some potential use cases for AAVE protocol?

Some potential use cases for AAVE protocol include cryptocurrency lending and borrowing, stablecoin lending and borrowing, serving as a decentralized borrowing and lending platform, providing liquidity to DeFi protocols, and creating decentralized insurance products.

How does AAVE protocol differ from traditional financial institutions?

AAVE protocol is decentralized and uses smart contracts and a decentralized governance model, whereas traditional financial institutions are centralized and typically operate through a hierarchical structure. AAVE protocol also allows for fast and secure transactions that are transparent and can be easily verified on the blockchain, whereas traditional financial institutions may have slower and less secure processes. Additionally, AAVE protocol is open and permissionless, meaning anyone can access and use the platform, whereas traditional financial institutions may have stricter requirements for access to financial services.

HOW AAVE PROTOCOL DIFFERS FROM OTHER DEFI PROTOCOLS

As the decentralized finance (DeFi) ecosystem continues to grow and evolve, a wide range of DeFi protocols have emerged, each offering its own unique set of features and functionality. In this article, we'll take a look at how AAVE protocol differs from other DeFi protocols and why it stands out in the DeFi landscape.

Introduction to DeFi Protocols

DeFi protocols are decentralized platforms that allow users to access financial services in a fast, secure, and transparent manner, without the need for a traditional financial institution. DeFi protocols are built on blockchain technology and use smart contracts to automate the process of lending and borrowing, enabling users to earn interest on their idle assets or borrow assets they need.

DeFi protocols offer a wide range of features and functionality, including lending and borrowing, liquidity provision, stablecoin issuance, and more. Some popular DeFi protocols include Compound, MakerDAO, and Uniswap.

How AAVE Protocol Differs from Other DeFi Protocols

While AAVE protocol shares many features and functionality with other DeFi protocols, there are a few key differences that set AAVE protocol apart:

- Asset coverage: One key difference between AAVE protocol and other DeFi protocols is the range of assets that can be lent and borrowed on the platform. AAVE protocol supports a wide range of assets, including cryptocurrencies such as Bitcoin and Ethereum, as well as stablecoins like DAI and USDC. In comparison, other DeFi protocols may only support a limited range of assets.
- Liquidation and collateral: AAVE protocol uses a system of liquidation and collateral to protect lenders in the event that a borrower defaults on their loan. If a borrower's collateral falls below a certain value, the AAVE protocol will automatically sell off the collateral to pay back the loan, minimizing losses for the lender. Other DeFi protocols may not have a similar system in place to protect lenders.
- Governance and staking: AAVE protocol uses a decentralized governance model that allows the AAVE community to collectively decide on important protocol updates and changes. Users can participate in governance by staking their AAVE tokens, which gives them voting rights and the ability to propose and vote on governance proposals. Other DeFi protocols may have different governance models, such as a centralized governance

structure or a hybrid model.

Why AAVE Protocol Stands Out in the DeFi Landscape

AAVE protocol's wide range of asset coverage, liquidation and collateral system, and decentralized governance model make it a unique and powerful DeFi protocol. These features, along with its strong track record of security and reliability, have helped AAVE protocol to stand out in the DeFi landscape and earn the trust of users.

In addition, AAVE protocol's focus on innovation and community engagement have helped it to stay at the forefront of the DeFi ecosystem. AAVE protocol has a strong track record of introducing new features and functionality, such as its support for flash loans, which allows users to borrow and repay a large amount of assets in a single transaction. AAVE protocol's commitment to the DeFi community is also evident in its active participation in DeFi events and its support for DeFi projects and initiatives.

Conclusion

AAVE protocol is a leading DeFi protocol that stands out in the DeFi landscape due to its wide range of asset coverage, liquidation and collateral system, decentralized governance model, and commitment to innovation and community engagement. If you're looking to get involved in DeFi and want a reliable and feature-rich platform, AAVE protocol is a great choice.

Exercises

To review these concepts, we will go through a series of exercises designed to test your understanding and apply what you have learned.

What is a DeFi protocol?
What are some key differences between AAVE protocol and other DeFi protocols?
What is AAVE protocol's liquidation and collateral system?
How does AAVE protocol's governance model differ from other DeFi protocols?
Why has AAVE protocol been successful in the DeFi landscape?

Solutions

What is a DeFi protocol?
A DeFi protocol is a decentralized platform that allows users to access financial services in a fast, secure, and transparent manner, without the need for a traditional financial institution. DeFi protocols are built on blockchain technology and use smart contracts to automate the process of lending and borrowing, enabling users to earn interest on their idle assets or borrow assets they need.

What are some key differences between AAVE protocol and other DeFi protocols?
Some key differences between AAVE protocol and other DeFi protocols include asset coverage, liquidation and collateral, and governance and staking.

What is AAVE protocol's liquidation and collateral system?
AAVE protocol's liquidation and collateral system is designed to protect lenders in the event that

a borrower defaults on their loan. If a borrower's collateral falls below a certain value, the AAVE protocol will automatically sell off the collateral to pay back the loan, minimizing losses for the lender.

How does AAVE protocol's governance model differ from other DeFi protocols?

AAVE protocol uses a decentralized governance model that allows the AAVE community to collectively decide on important protocol updates and changes. Users can participate in governance by staking their AAVE tokens, which gives them voting rights and the ability to propose and vote on governance proposals. Other DeFi protocols may have different governance models, such as a centralized governance structure or a hybrid model.

Why has AAVE protocol been successful in the DeFi landscape?

AAVE protocol has been successful in the DeFi landscape due to its wide range of asset coverage, liquidation and collateral system, decentralized governance model, and commitment to innovation and community engagement. Its strong track record of security and reliability, along with its focus on introducing new features and functionality, has helped AAVE protocol to stand out in the DeFi ecosystem.

INSTALLING DEPENDENCIES
AND TOOLS

Before you can start building decentralized finance (DeFi) applications using AAVE protocol, you'll need to set up your development environment and install the necessary dependencies and tools. In this article, we'll walk you through the process of installing and configuring everything you need to get started with AAVE protocol.

Prerequisites

Before you begin, it's important to make sure you have the following prerequisites in place:

- A computer with an internet connection
- A text editor or code editor (such as Visual Studio Code)
- Basic knowledge of the command line and JavaScript

If you don't already have these things, take some time to set them up before proceeding.

Installing Node.js and npm

The first thing you'll need to do is install Node.js and npm, which are required to run JavaScript code on your computer. Node.js is a JavaScript runtime that allows you to execute JavaScript code outside of a web browser, while npm is a package manager that makes it easy to install and manage Node.js packages.

To install Node.js and npm, follow these steps:

1. Go to the Node.js website (https://nodejs.org/) and click the "Download" button to download the latest version of Node.js.
2. Run the downloaded installer file and follow the prompts to install Node.js and npm.
3. To verify that Node.js and npm are installed correctly, open a command prompt or terminal window and type the following commands:

```
node -v
```
```
npm -v
```

The output should show the version number of Node.js and npm that you have installed.

Installing Truffle

Next, you'll need to install Truffle, which is a popular development framework for Ethereum. Truffle provides a suite of tools and libraries that make it easy to build and deploy smart contracts and decentralized applications (DApps) on the Ethereum blockchain.

To install Truffle, follow these steps:

1. Open a command prompt or terminal window and type the following command:

```
npm install -g truffle
```

This will install Truffle globally on your system, allowing you to use it from any directory.

2. To verify that Truffle is installed correctly, type the following command:

```
truffle version
```

Installing MetaMask

MetaMask is a browser extension that allows you to interact with the Ethereum blockchain from your web browser. It's an essential tool for any Ethereum developer, as it allows you to test your DApps, sign transactions, and manage your Ethereum accounts.

To install MetaMask, follow these steps:

1. Go to the MetaMask website (https://metamask.io/) and click the "Get MetaMask" button.
2. Select your web browser (Chrome, Firefox, etc.) and click the "Add to [browser]" button to add the MetaMask extension to your browser.
3. Click the "Add Extension" button to confirm the installation.
4. Once MetaMask is installed, click the MetaMask icon in your browser's toolbar to open the MetaMask extension.
5. Follow the prompts to create a new Ethereum account and set up your MetaMask wallet.

Installing AAVE Protocol Dependencies

To use AAVE protocol in your DApps, you'll need to install the aave-js library, which is a JavaScript library for interacting with AAVE protocol.

To install the aave-js library, follow these steps:

1. Create a new directory for your project and navigate to it in your command prompt or terminal window.
2. Type the following command to initialize a new npm project:

```
npm init -y
```

This will create a package.json file in your project directory.

3. Type the following command to install the aave-js library as a dependency:

This will install the aave-js library and add it to your project's dependencies in the package.json file.

Congratulations! You have now installed all of the dependencies and tools you need to start building DeFi applications using AAVE protocol. Next, let's take a look at how to use the aave-js library to interact with AAVE protocol.

Using the aave-js Library

Now that you have installed the aave-js library, you can start using it to interact with AAVE protocol from your DApps. Here are some examples of how you can use the aave-js library:

- Connecting to AAVE protocol: To connect to AAVE protocol, you can use the Aave.createInstance() method, which returns an instance of the AAVE client. For example:

```
const Aave = require('@aave/aave-js');
const aave = Aave.createInstance();
```

- Checking the balance of an account: To check the balance of an Ethereum account, you can use the getBalance() method, which returns the balance in wei. For example:

```
const balance = await aave.getBalance('0x1234567890abcdef');
console.log(balance); // 1234567890
```

- Lending and borrowing assets: To lend or borrow assets on AAVE protocol, you can use the lend() and borrow() methods, respectively. For example:

```
await aave.lend('DAI', '100000000'); // lend 100 DAI
await aave.borrow('DAI', '100000000'); // borrow 100 DAI
```

These are just a few examples of how you can use the aave-js library to interact with AAVE protocol. For a complete list of available methods and more detailed documentation, you can refer to the aave-js library documentation (https://aave.com/developers/docs/aave-js).

Conclusion

In this article, we've covered the steps you need to take to install and set up your development environment for building DeFi applications using AAVE protocol. We've also introduced the aave-js library, which you can use to interact with AAVE protocol from your DApps. With these tools and dependencies in place, you're now ready to start building DeFi applications with AAVE protocol.

Exercises

To review these concepts, we will go through a series of exercises designed to test your understanding and apply what you have learned.

What are the prerequisites for setting up a development environment for AAVE protocol?
How do you install Node.js and npm?
How do you install Truffle?
How do you install MetaMask?
How do you install the aave-js library?

Solutions

What are the prerequisites for setting up a development environment for AAVE protocol?
The prerequisites for setting up a development environment for AAVE protocol include a computer with an internet connection, a text editor or code editor, and basic knowledge of the command line

and JavaScript.

How do you install Node.js and npm?

To install Node.js and npm, go to the Node.js website (**https://nodejs.org/**) and click the "Download" button to download the latest version of Node.js. Then, run the downloaded installer file and follow the prompts to install Node.js and npm.

How do you install Truffle?

To install Truffle, open a command prompt or terminal window and type the following command:

```
npm install -g truffle
```

How do you install MetaMask?

To install MetaMask, go to the MetaMask website (**https://metamask.io/**) and click the "Get MetaMask" button. Select your web browser and click the "Add to [browser]" button to add the MetaMask extension to your browser. Click the "Add Extension" button to confirm the installation. Once MetaMask is installed, click the MetaMask icon in your browser's toolbar to open the MetaMask extension and follow the prompts to create a new Ethereum account and set up your MetaMask wallet.

How do you install the aave-js library?

To install the aave-js library, create a new directory for your project and navigate to it in your command prompt or terminal window. Then, type the following command to initialize a new npm project:

```
npm init -y
```

Next, type the following command to install the aave-js library as a dependency:

```
npm install @aave/aave-js
```

SETTING UP A LOCAL AAVE TEST ENVIRONMENT

As a decentralized finance (DeFi) developer, it's important to test your applications and smart contracts before deploying them to the main Ethereum network. To do this, you can set up a local test environment using AAVE protocol, which allows you to simulate the behavior of the AAVE protocol on a local Ethereum network.

In this article, we'll walk you through the process of setting up a local AAVE test environment, including how to install and configure the necessary dependencies and tools.

Prerequisites
Before you begin, make sure you have the following prerequisites in place:

- A computer with an internet connection
- Node.js and npm installed (see the previous lesson for instructions)
- Truffle installed (see the previous lesson for instructions)
- MetaMask installed and configured (see the previous lesson for instructions)

Installing Ganache
To set up a local Ethereum network, you'll need to install Ganache, which is a local blockchain tool that allows you to run your own private Ethereum network.

To install Ganache, follow these steps:

1. Go to the Ganache website (https://www.trufflesuite.com/ganache) and click the "Download" button to download the latest version of Ganache.
2. Run the downloaded installer file and follow the prompts to install Ganache.
3. Once Ganache is installed, launch the application and click the "Quickstart" button to create a new workspace.
4. In the "New Workspace" dialog, give your workspace a name and click the "Create Workspace" button.
5. Ganache will now create a new private Ethereum network for you to use for testing.

Connecting MetaMask to Ganache
Once you have Ganache set up, you'll need to connect MetaMask to your local Ethereum network so that you can interact with it from your web browser. To do this, follow these steps:

1. Click the MetaMask icon in your browser's toolbar to open the MetaMask extension.
2. In the MetaMask window, click the "Network" dropdown and select "Custom RPC".

3. In the "New RPC URL" field, enter the following URL: http://127.0.0.1:7545
4. Click the "Save" button to add the custom RPC to your MetaMask network list.
5. In the MetaMask window, click the "Accounts" tab and then click the "Import Account" button.
6. In the "Private Key" field, enter the private key for one of the accounts listed in the Ganache accounts table. You can find the private keys by clicking the "Key" icon next to each account in the Ganache accounts table.
7. Click the "Import" button to import the account into MetaMask.

You should now be connected to your local Ethereum network in MetaMask. You can verify this by checking the network name in the MetaMask window, which should show "Private Network".

Installing the AAVE Protocol Smart Contracts

To use AAVE protocol on your local Ethereum network, you'll need to deploy the AAVE protocol smart contracts to your local chain. To do this, follow these steps:

1. Clone the AAVE protocol repository from GitHub:

```
git clone https://github.com/aave/aave-protocol.git
```

2. Navigate to the aave-protocol directory and install the required dependencies:

```
cd aave-protocol
```
```
npm install
```

3. Compile the smart contracts:

```
truffle compile
```

4. Migrate the smart contracts to your local Ethereum network:

```
truffle migrate
```

This will deploy the AAVE protocol smart contracts to your local Ethereum network.

Using AAVE Protocol on Your Local Network

Now that you have AAVE protocol deployed on your local Ethereum network, you can start using it to test your DeFi applications. To do this, you'll need to use the aave-js library (https://aave.com/developers/docs/aave-js) to interact with AAVE protocol from your DApps.

For example, you can use the Aave.createInstance() method to connect to AAVE protocol, and then use the lend() and borrow() methods to lend and borrow assets, respectively. You can also use the getBalance()method to check the balance of an Ethereum account on AAVE protocol.

Conclusion

In this article, we've covered the steps you need to take to set up a local AAVE test environment for testing your DeFi applications and smart contracts. By using a local Ethereum network and AAVE protocol, you can simulate the behavior of the AAVE protocol and test your applications in a safe and controlled environment before deploying them to the main Ethereum network.

Exercises

To review these concepts, we will go through a series of exercises designed to test your understanding and apply what you have learned.

What is Ganache and what is it used for?
How do you connect MetaMask to a local Ethereum network using Ganache?
How do you install the AAVE protocol smart contracts on a local Ethereum network?
How do you connect to AAVE protocol using the aave-js library?
How do you lend and borrow assets using the aave-js library?

Solutions

What is Ganache and what is it used for?
Ganache is a local blockchain tool that allows you to run your own private Ethereum network. It is used to create a local Ethereum network for testing purposes.

How do you connect MetaMask to a local Ethereum network using Ganache?
To connect MetaMask to a local Ethereum network using Ganache, click the MetaMask icon in your browser's toolbar to open the MetaMask extension. In the MetaMask window, click the "Network" dropdown and select "Custom RPC". In the "New RPC URL" field, enter the following URL: http://127.0.0.1:7545. Click the "Save" button to add the custom RPC to your MetaMask network list. In the MetaMask window, click the "Accounts" tab and then click the "Import Account" button. In the "Private Key" field, enter the private key for one of the accounts listed in the Ganache accounts table. Click the "Import" button to import the account into MetaMask.

How do you install the AAVE protocol smart contracts on a local Ethereum network?
o install the AAVE protocol smart contracts on a local Ethereum network, clone the AAVE protocol repository from GitHub:

```
git clone https://github.com/aave/aave-protocol.git
```

Next, navigate to the aave-protocol directory and install the required dependencies:

```
cd aave-protocol
```
```
npm install
```

Then, compile the smart contracts:

```
truffle compile
```

Finally, migrate the smart contracts to your local Ethereum network:

```
truffle migrate
```

How do you connect to AAVE protocol using the aave-js library?
To connect to AAVE protocol using the aave-js library, use the Aave.createInstance() method, which returns an instance of the AAVE client. For example:

```
const Aave = require('@aave/aave-js');
```
```
const aave = Aave.createInstance();
```

How do you lend and borrow assets using the aave-js library?

To lend or borrow assets using the a aave-js library, use the lend()and borrow() methods, respectively. These methods take two arguments: the asset to lend or borrow (in the form of a symbol or contract address), and the amount to lend or borrow (in wei). For example:

```
await aave.lend('DAI', '100000000'); // lend 100 DAI
```

```
await aave.borrow('DAI', '100000000'); // borrow 100 DAI
```

Note that you'll need to have sufficient balance in your Ethereum account in order to lend or borrow assets. You can check your balance using the getBalance() method:

```
const balance = await aave.getBalance('0x1234567890abcdef');
```

```
console.log(balance); // 1234567890
```

OVERVIEW OF THE AAVE PROTOCOL ARCHITECTURE

As a decentralized finance (DeFi) developer, it's important to understand the underlying architecture of the protocols you're working with. In this article, we'll provide a detailed overview of the AAVE protocol architecture, which is a decentralized lending and borrowing platform built on Ethereum.

The AAVE protocol is designed to allow users to lend and borrow a variety of assets, including cryptocurrencies and stablecoins, using smart contracts. It utilizes a unique liquidity pool model, which allows users to earn interest on their deposited assets and borrow assets at competitive rates.

In this article, we'll explore the key components of the AAVE protocol architecture in greater detail, including the liquidity pools, the lending and borrowing mechanics, and the role of the Aave token. We'll also provide examples of how to interact with the AAVE protocol using the aave-js library.

Liquidity Pools

At the heart of the AAVE protocol is a system of liquidity pools, which are pools of assets that are available for lending and borrowing. Users can deposit their assets into these pools, and in return, they'll receive a share of the pool in the form of a token.

For example, if you deposit 100 DAI into the DAI liquidity pool, you'll receive a certain number of DAI pool tokens in return. These pool tokens represent your share of the pool and can be traded on exchanges or used to borrow or lend assets.

The AAVE protocol currently supports a variety of liquidity pools, including pools for popular cryptocurrencies such as Ethereum (ETH) and Bitcoin (BTC), as well as stablecoins such as DAI and USDC.

To deposit assets into a liquidity pool using the aave-js library, you can use the deposit() method. For example, to deposit 100 DAI into the DAI liquidity pool, you can use the following code:

```
const Aave = require('@aave/aave-js');
const aave = Aave.createInstance();
await aave.deposit('DAI', '100000000'); // deposit 100 DAI
```

Lending and Borrowing Mechanics

The AAVE protocol uses a unique lending and borrowing mechanism called "flash loans", which allows users to borrow assets instantly and repay them within the same transaction. This allows users to borrow and lend assets in a fast and efficient manner, without the need for collateral.

To borrow assets, a user simply needs to send a request to the AAVE protocol with the desired amount and asset, and the protocol will automatically transfer the assets to the user's Ethereum account. The user can then repay the loan by returning the borrowed assets to the protocol within the same transaction.

To borrow assets using the aave-js library, you can use the borrow()method. For example, to borrow 100 DAI from the DAI liquidity pool, you can use the following code:

```
await aave.borrow('DAI', '100000000'); // borrow 100 DAI
```

To repay a loan, you can use the repay() method. For example, to repay the above loan of 100 DAI, you can use the following code:

```
await aave.repay('DAI', '100000000'); // repay 100 DAI
```

It's worth noting that the AAVE protocol imposes certain limits on flash loans, such as a maximum loan amount and a maximum interest rate. These limits are designed to protect the protocol from malicious attacks and ensure the stability of the system.

Aave Token

The Aave token (AAVE) is the native token of the AAVE protocol and serves several important functions within the protocol's architecture.

First, AAVE is used as a governance token, allowing token holders to vote on protocol updates and governance decisions. Token holders can submit proposals for changes to the protocol, and if a proposal receives a sufficient number of votes, it will be implemented.

Second, AAVE is used as a staking token, allowing users to earn rewards by staking their AAVE tokens and participating in the protocol's liquidity pools. Users who stake their AAVE tokens can earn a share of the fees collected by the protocol, as well as a portion of the interest earned on deposited assets.

To stake AAVE tokens using the aave-js library, you can use the stake()method. For example, to stake 100 AAVE tokens in the AAVE liquidity pool, you can use the following code:

```
await aave.stake('AAVE', '100000000'); // stake 100 AAVE
```

Finally, AAVE is used as a collateral token, allowing users to collateralize their loans and borrow at lower rates. When borrowing assets, users have the option to provide collateral in the form of AAVE tokens. If the value of the borrowed assets falls below a certain threshold (known as the "liquidation threshold"), the AAVE tokens will be sold to repay the loan.

To provide AAVE tokens as collateral for a loan using the aave-js library, you can use the provideCollateral() method. For example, to provide 100 AAVE tokens as collateral for a DAI loan, you can use the following code:

```
// provide 100 AAVE as collateral for a DAI loan
```
```
await aave.provideCollateral('DAI', '100000000');
```

Conclusion

In this article, we've provided a detailed overview of the AAVE protocol architecture and its key components. By understanding the liquidity pools, lending and borrowing mechanics, and the role of the Aave token, you'll be better equipped to build DeFi applications on top of the AAVE protocol. We've also provided examples of how to interact with the AAVE protocol using the aave-js library.

Exercises

To review these concepts, we will go through a series of exercises designed to test your understanding and apply what you have learned.

How do you deposit assets into a liquidity pool using the aave-js library?
How do you borrow assets from a liquidity pool using the aave-js library?
How do you repay a loan using the aave-js library?
How do you stake AAVE tokens in a liquidity pool using the aave-js library?
How do you provide AAVE tokens as collateral for a loan using the aave-js library?

Solutions

How do you deposit assets into a liquidity pool using the aave-js library?
To deposit assets into a liquidity pool using the aave-js library, use the deposit() method. This method takes two arguments: the asset to deposit (in the form of a symbol or contract address), and the amount to deposit (in wei). For example:

```
// deposit 100 DAI
```
```
await aave.deposit('DAI', '100000000');
```

How do you borrow assets from a liquidity pool using the aave-js library?
To borrow assets from a liquidity pool using the aave-js library, use the borrow() method. This method takes two arguments: the asset to borrow (in the form of a symbol or contract address), and the amount to borrow (in wei). For example:

```
// borrow 100 DAI
```
```
await aave.borrow('DAI', '100000000');
```

How do you repay a loan using the aave-js library?
To repay a loan using the aave-js library, use the repay() method. This method takes two arguments: the asset of the loan (in the form of a symbol or contract address), and the amount to repay (in wei). For example:

```
// repay 100 DAI
```
```
await aave.repay('DAI', '100000000');
```

How do you stake AAVE tokens in a liquidity pool using the aave-js library?

To stake AAVE tokens in a liquidity pool using the aave-js library, use the stake() method. This method takes two arguments: the asset to stake (in the form of a symbol or contract address), and the amount to stake (in wei). For example:

```
// stake 100 AAVE
await aave.stake('AAVE', '100000000');
```

How do you provide AAVE tokens as collateral for a loan using the aave-js library?

To provide AAVE tokens as collateral for a loan using the aave-js library, use the provideCollateral() method. This method takes two arguments: the asset of the loan (in the form of a symbol or contract address), and the amount of AAVE to provide as collateral (in wei). For example:

```
// provide 100 AAVE as collateral for a DAI loan
await aave.provideCollateral('DAI', '100000000');
```

KEY COMPONENTS OF THE AAVE PROTOCOL

As a decentralized finance (DeFi) developer, it's important to understand the key components of the protocols you're working with. In this article, we'll provide a detailed overview of the key components of the AAVE protocol, which is a decentralized lending and borrowing platform built on Ethereum.

The AAVE protocol is designed to allow users to lend and borrow a variety of assets, including cryptocurrencies and stablecoins, using smart contracts. It utilizes a unique liquidity pool model, which allows users to earn interest on their deposited assets and borrow assets at competitive rates.

In this article, we'll explore the various components of the AAVE protocol, including the interest rate models, the collateral system, and the safety measures. We'll also provide examples of how to interact with these components using the aave-js library.

Interest Rate Models

One of the key components of the AAVE protocol is the interest rate model, which determines the rate at which users can borrow and lend assets. The AAVE protocol currently supports three interest rate models: the stable rate model, the variable rate model, and the flash loan rate model.

The stable rate model is a fixed interest rate model, where the interest rate for a given asset is set at a constant rate. This model is suitable for stablecoins, which are designed to maintain a stable value.

To borrow or lend assets using the stable rate model using the aave-js library, you can use the borrowStable() and lendStable() methods, respectively. These methods take three arguments: the asset (in the form of a symbol or contract address), the amount to borrow or lend (in wei), and the duration of the loan (in seconds). For example:

```
await aave.borrowStable('DAI', '100000000', '86400');
// borrow 100 DAI for 1 day (86400 seconds)
await aave.lendStable('DAI', '100000000', '86400');
// lend 100 DAI for 1 day (86400 seconds)
```

The variable rate model is a variable interest rate model, where the interest rate for a given asset is determined by supply and demand. This model is suitable for cryptocurrencies, which can fluctuate in value.

To borrow or lend assets using the variable rate model using the aave-js library, you can use the borrowVariable() and lendVariable() methods, respectively. These methods take the same arguments as the borrowStable() and lendStable() methods, respectively. For example:

```
await aave.borrowVariable('ETH', '100000000', '86400');
// borrow 100 ETH for 1 day (86400 seconds)
await aave.lendVariable('ETH', '100000000', '86400');
// lend 100 ETH for 1 day (86400 seconds)
```

The flash loan rate model is a special interest rate model that is only available for flash loans. Flash loans are a unique feature of the AAVE protocol that allow users to borrow assets instantly and repay them within the same transaction. The flash loan rate model is designed to allow users to borrow and lend assets at a rate that reflects the risk of the flash loan.

To borrow assets using the flash loan rate model using the aave-js library, you can use the borrow() method. This method takes two arguments: the asset to borrow (in the form of a symbol or contract address), and the amount to borrow (in wei). For example:

```
await aave.borrow('DAI', '100000000');
// borrow 100 DAI
```

Note that flash loans do not have a corresponding "lend" method, as the assets are automatically returned to the protocol within the same transaction.

Collateral System

Another key component of the AAVE protocol is the collateral system, which allows users to collateralize their loans and borrow at lower rates. When borrowing assets, users have the option to provide collateral in the form of AAVE tokens or other supported assets. If the value of the borrowed assets falls below a certain threshold (known as the "liquidation threshold"), the collateral will be sold to repay the loan.

To provide collateral for a loan using the aave-js library, you can use the provideCollateral() method. This method takes two arguments: the asset of the loan (in the form of a symbol or contract address), and the amount of collateral to provide (in wei). For example:

```
await aave.provideCollateral('DAI', '100000000');
// provide 100 AAVE as collateral for a DAI loan
```

It's worth noting that the AAVE protocol imposes certain requirements on the collateral system, such as a minimum collateralization ratio (the ratio of the collateral value to the loan value) and a maximum loan-to-value ratio (the ratio of the loan value to the collateral value). These requirements are designed to protect the protocol from potential losses and ensure the stability of the system.

Safety Measures

The AAVE protocol includes several safety measures to protect the protocol and its users from potential risks. One of these measures is the emergency stop mechanism, which allows the protocol to be temporarily suspended in the event of a critical issue.

To trigger the emergency stop mechanism using the aave-js library, you can use the emergencyStop() method. This method takes no arguments and returns a boolean value indicating whether the emergency stop was successful. For example:

```
const success = await aave.emergencyStop();
// trigger the emergency stop mechanism
```

Another safety measure is the liquidation mechanism, which is activated when the value of a borrower's collateral falls below the liquidation threshold. When a borrower's collateral is liquidated, their loan is automatically repaid and the collateral is sold to cover any losses.

To trigger the liquidation mechanism using the aave-js library, you can use the liquidate() method. This method takes two arguments: the asset of the loan (in the form of a symbol or contract address) and the borrower's Ethereum address. For example:

```
await aave.liquidate('DAI', '0x...');
// trigger the liquidation mechanism for a
// DAI loan belonging to the specified borrower
```

Finally, the AAVE protocol includes a system for handling undercollateralized loans, which are loans that have a collateralization ratio below the minimum required by the protocol. When an undercollateralized loan is detected, the AAVE protocol will automatically sell a portion of the borrower's collateral to bring the loan back above the minimum collateralization ratio.

To handle undercollateralized loans using the aave-js library, you can use the handleUndercollateralizedLoans() method. This method takes no arguments and returns a boolean value indicating whether the undercollateralized loans were successfully handled. For example:

```
const success = await
aave.handleUndercollateralizedLoans();
// handle undercollateralized loans
```

Conclusion

In this article, we've explored the key components of the AAVE protocol, including the interest rate models, the collateral system, and the safety measures. By understanding these components, you'll be better equipped to build DeFi applications on top of the AAVE protocol. We've also provided examples of how to interact with these components using the aave-js library.

Exercises

To review these concepts, we will go through a series of exercises designed to test your understanding and apply what you have learned.

How do you borrow assets using the stable rate model using the aave-js library?
How do you lend assets using the stable rate model using the aave-js library?
How do you borrow assets using the variable rate model using the aave-js library?

How do you lend assets using the variable rate model using the aave-js library?

How do you borrow assets using the flash loan rate model using the aave-js library?

Solutions

How do you borrow assets using the stable rate model using the aave-js library?

To borrow assets using the stable rate model using the aave-js library, use the borrowStable() method. This method takes three arguments: the asset to borrow (in the form of a symbol or contract address), the amount to borrow (in wei), and the duration of the loan (in seconds). For example:

```
await aave.borrowStable('DAI', '100000000', '86400');
// borrow 100 DAI for 1 day (86400 seconds)
```

How do you lend assets using the stable rate model using the aave-js library?

To lend assets using the stable rate model using the aave-js library, use the lendStable() method. This method takes the same arguments as the borrowStable() method. For example:

```
await aave.lendStable('DAI', '100000000', '86400');
// lend 100 DAI for 1 day (86400 seconds)
```

How do you borrow assets using the variable rate model using the aave-js library?

To borrow assets using the variable rate model using the aave-js library, use the borrowVariable() method. This method takes the same arguments as the borrowStable() method. For example:

```
await aave.borrowVariable('ETH', '100000000', '86400');
// borrow 100 ETH for 1 day (86400 seconds)
```

How do you lend assets using the variable rate model using the aave-js library?

To lend assets using the variable rate model using the aave-js library, use the lendVariable() method. This method takes the same arguments as the lendStable() method. For example:

```
await aave.lendVariable('ETH', '100000000', '86400');
// lend 100 ETH for 1 day (86400 seconds)
```

How do you borrow assets using the flash loan rate model using the aave-js library?

To borrow assets using the flash loan rate model using the aave-js library, use the borrow() method. This method takes two arguments: the asset to borrow (in the form of a symbol or contract address), and the amount to borrow (in wei). For example:

```
await aave.borrow('DAI', '100000000');
// borrow 100 DAI
```

Note that flash loans do not have a corresponding "lend" method, as the assets are automatically returned to the protocol within the same transaction.

UNDERSTANDING THE DIFFERENT TYPES OF SMART CONTRACTS IN AAVE PROTOCOL

As a decentralized finance (DeFi) developer, it's important to understand the different types of smart contracts that make up the AAVE protocol. In this article, we'll provide a detailed overview of the different types of smart contracts in AAVE and how they work. We'll also provide examples of how to interact with these contracts using the aave-js library.

The AAVE protocol is built on Ethereum and consists of a series of smart contracts that enable lending and borrowing functionality. These smart contracts can be grouped into three main categories: the lending pool contracts, the price oracle contracts, and the market contracts.

Lending Pool Contracts

The lending pool contracts are the core of the AAVE protocol and are responsible for managing the lending and borrowing of assets. Each asset has its own lending pool contract, which tracks the supply and demand for that asset and determines the interest rates.

To interact with the lending pool contracts using the aave-js library, you can use the getLendingPool() method. This method takes an asset symbol or contract address as an argument and returns an instance of the LendingPool contract for that asset. You can then use the methods of the LendingPool contract to interact with the lending pool.

For example, to get the total supply of an asset in the lending pool, you can use the totalSupply() method:

```
const lendingPool = await aave.getLendingPool('DAI');
// get the DAI lending pool contract
const totalSupply = await lendingPool.totalSupply();
// get the total supply of DAI in the lending pool
```

To get the current interest rate for an asset in the lending pool, you can use the getCurrentVariableInterestRate() method:

```
const lendingPool = await aave.getLendingPool('ETH');
// get the ETH lending pool contract
const interestRate = await lendingPool.getCurrentVariableInterestRate();
```

```
// get the current interest rate for ETH
```

Price Oracle Contracts

The price oracle contracts are responsible for providing the current prices of assets to the lending pool contracts. These prices are used to determine the value of collateral and the liquidation threshold for loans.

To interact with the price oracle contracts using the aave-js library, you can use the getPriceOracle() method. This method takes an asset symbol or contract address as an argument and returns an instance of the PriceOracle contract for that asset. You can then use the methods of the PriceOracle contract to interact with the price oracle.

For example, to get the current price of an asset in the price oracle, you can use the getCurrentPrice() method:

```
const priceOracle = await aave.getPriceOracle('DAI');
// get the DAI price oracle contract
const currentPrice = await priceOracle.getCurrentPrice();
// get the current price of DAI
```

To get the minimum collateralization ratio for an asset in the price oracle, you can use the getMinimumCollateralizationRatio() method:

```
const priceOracle = await aave.getPriceOracle('ETH');
// get the ETH price oracle contract
const minCollateralizationRatio = await priceOracle.getMinimumCollateralizationRatio();
// get the minimum collateralization ratio for ETH
```

Market Contracts

The market contracts are responsible for managing the sale and purchase of assets in the AAVE protocol. These contracts allow users to buy and sell assets using the AAVE token as a medium of exchange.

To interact with the market contracts using the aave-js library, you can use the getMarket() method. This method takes an asset symbol or contract address as an argument and returns an instance of the Market contract for that asset. You can then use the methods of the Market contract to interact with the market.

For example, to buy an asset in the market using the aave-js library, you can use the buy() method. This method takes two arguments: the asset to buy (in the form of a symbol or contract address), and the amount of AAVE to spend (in wei). For example:

```
const market = await aave.getMarket('DAI');
// get the DAI market contract
await market.buy('DAI', '100000000');
```

```
// buy 100 DAI using AAVE
```

To sell an asset in the market using the aave-js library, you can use the sell() method. This method takes the same arguments as the buy()method. For example:

```
const market = await aave.getMarket('ETH');
// get the ETH market contract
await market.sell('ETH', '100000000');
// sell 100 ETH for AAVE
```

Conclusion

In this article, we've explored the different types of smart contracts in the AAVE protocol and provided examples of how to interact with them using the aave-js library. Understanding these smart contracts is key to building DeFi applications on top of the AAVE protocol.

Exercises

To review these concepts, we will go through a series of exercises designed to test your understanding and apply what you have learned.

How do you get the total supply of an asset in the lending pool using the aave-js library?
How do you get the current interest rate for an asset in the lending pool using the aave-js library?
How do you get the current price of an asset in the price oracle using the aave-js library?
How do you get the minimum collateralization ratio for an asset in the price oracle using the aave-js library?
How do you sell an asset in the market using the aave-js library?

Solutions

How do you get the total supply of an asset in the lending pool using the aave-js library?
To get the total supply of an asset in the lending pool using the aave-js library, use the getLendingPool() method to get the LendingPool contract for the asset, and then use the totalSupply() method of the LendingPool contract. For example:

```
const lendingPool = await aave.getLendingPool('DAI');
// get the DAI lending pool contract
const totalSupply = await lendingPool.totalSupply();
// get the total supply of DAI in the lending pool
```

How do you get the current interest rate for an asset in the lending pool using the aave-js library?
To get the current interest rate for an asset in the lending pool using the aave-js library, use the getLendingPool() method to get the LendingPool contract for the asset, and then use the getCurrentVariableInterestRate() method of the LendingPool contract. For example:

```
const lendingPool = await aave.getLendingPool('ETH');
// get the ETH lending pool contract
```

```
const interestRate = await lendingPool.getCurrentVariableInterestRate();
// get the current interest rate for ETH
```

How do you get the current price of an asset in the price oracle using the aave-js library?

To get the current price of an asset in the price oracle using the aave-js library, use the getPriceOracle() method to get the PriceOracle contract for the asset, and then use the getCurrentPrice() method of the PriceOracle contract. For example:

```
const priceOracle = await aave.getPriceOracle('DAI');
// get the DAI price oracle contract
const currentPrice = await priceOracle.getCurrentPrice();
// get the current price of DAI
```

How do you get the minimum collateralization ratio for an asset in the price oracle using the aave-js library?

To get the minimum collateralization ratio for an asset in the price oracle using the aave-js library, use the getPriceOracle() method to get the PriceOracle contract for the asset, and then use the getMinimumCollateralizationRatio() method of the PriceOracle contract. For example:

```
const priceOracle = await aave.getPriceOracle('ETH');
// get the ETH price oracle contract
const minCollateralizationRatio = await priceOracle.getMinimumCollateralizationRatio();
// get the minimum collateralization ratio for ETH
```

How do you sell an asset in the market using the aave-js library?

To sell an asset in the market using the aave-js library, use the getMarket() method to get the Market contract for the asset, and then use the sell() method of the Market contract. This method takes two arguments: the asset to sell (in the form of a symbol or contract address), and the amount of AAVE to receive (in wei). For example:

```
const market = await aave.getMarket('ETH');
// get the ETH market contract
await market.sell('ETH', '100000000');
// sell 100 ETH for AAVE
```

Note that you will need to have the asset you want to sell in your wallet and have approved the Market contract to transfer it. You can do this using the approve() method of the ERC20 contract for the asset. For example:

```
const erc20 = new web3.eth.Contract(ERC20_ABI, '0xEeeeeEeeeEeEeeEeEeEeeEEEeeeeEeeeeeeeEEeE');
// get the ERC20 contract for the asset
await         erc20.methods.approve('0xAAveMarketAddress',         '100000000').send({         from:
'0xMyWalletAddress' });
// approve the Market contract to transfer 100 of the asset
```

INTERACTING WITH AAVE SMART CONTRACTS USING WEB3

As a blockchain developer, you may want to interact directly with the AAVE smart contracts using the Web3 library. In this article, we'll provide a detailed guide on how to do this, including examples of common actions such as lending and borrowing assets, getting the current interest rates, and checking the balance of a contract.

Before we begin, make sure you have a Web3 provider set up and connected to the Ethereum network. You can use a local Ethereum node such as Ganache, or a public node such as Infura. You'll also need the ABI (Application Binary Interface) and contract addresses of the AAVE smart contracts you want to interact with. You can find these in the AAVE documentation.

Lending and Borrowing Assets

To lend or borrow assets using the AAVE smart contracts, you'll need to use the LendingPool contract for the asset. The LendingPool contract has methods for lending and borrowing both stable (fixed rate) and variable (market rate) loans.

To lend an asset using the stable rate model, you can use the lendStable() method of the LendingPool contract. This method takes three arguments: the asset to lend (in the form of a contract address), the amount to lend (in wei), and the duration of the loan (in seconds). For example:

```
const lendingPool = new web3.eth.Contract(LendingPool_ABI, '0xAAveLendingPoolAddress'); // get the
LendingPool contract
await lendingPool.methods.lendStable('0xDAIContractAddress', '100000000', '86400').send({ from:
'0xMyWalletAddress' }); // lend 100 DAI for 1 day (86400 seconds)
```

To borrow an asset using the stable rate model, you can use the borrowStable() method of the LendingPool contract. This method takes the same arguments as the lendStable() method. For example:

```
const lendingPool = new web3.eth.Contract(LendingPool_ABI, '0xAAveLendingPoolAddress'); // get the
LendingPool contract
await lendingPool.methods.borrowStable('0xDAIContractAddress', '100000000', '86400').send({ from:
'0xMyWalletAddress' }); // borrow 100 DAI for 1 day (86400 seconds)
```

To lend an asset using the variable rate model, you can use the lendVariable() method of the LendingPool contract. This method takes two arguments: the asset to lend (in the form of a contract address), and the amount to lend (in wei). For example:

```
const lendingPool = new web3.eth.Contract(LendingPool_ABI, '0xAAveLendingPoolAddress'); // get the
LendingPool contract
```

```
await     lendingPool.methods.lendVariable('0xETHContractAddress',     '100000000').send({     from:
'0xMyWalletAddress' }); // lend 100 ETH
```

To borrow an asset using the variable rate model, you can use the borrowVariable() method of the LendingPool contract. This method takes the same arguments as the lendVariable() method. For example:

```
const lendingPool = new web3.eth.Contract(LendingPool_ABI, '0xAAveLendingPoolAddress'); // get the
LendingPool contract
```

```
await     lendingPool.methods.borrowVariable('0xETHContractAddress',     '100000000').send({     from:
'0xMyWalletAddress' }); // borrow 100 ETH
```

Getting Interest Rates

To get the current interest rate for an asset in the lending pool, you can use the getCurrentVariableInterestRate() method of the LendingPool contract. This method takes no arguments and returns the current interest rate as a BigNumber object. For example:

```
const lendingPool = new web3.eth.Contract(LendingPool_ABI, '0xAAveLendingPoolAddress'); // get the
LendingPool contract
```

```
const interestRate = await lendingPool.methods.getCurrentVariableInterestRate().call(); // get the
current interest rate for the asset
```

To get the minimum collateralization ratio for an asset in the price oracle, you can use the getMinimumCollateralizationRatio() method of the PriceOracle contract. This method takes no arguments and returns the minimum collateralization ratio as a BigNumber object. For example:

```
const priceOracle = new web3.eth.Contract(PriceOracle_ABI, '0xAAvePriceOracleAddress'); // get the
PriceOracle contract
```

```
const               minCollateralizationRatio               =               await
priceOracle.methods.getMinimumCollateralizationRatio().call(); // get the minimum collateralization
ratio for the asset
```

Checking Balances

To check the balance of a contract or wallet address, you can use the balanceOf() method of the ERC20 contract for the asset. This method takes an address as an argument and returns the balance of that address as a BigNumber object. For example:

```
const erc20 = new web3.eth.Contract(ERC20_ABI, '0xEeeeeEeeeEeEeeEeEeEeeEEEeeeeEeeeeeeeEEeE'); //
get the ERC20 contract for the asset
```

```
const balance = await erc20.methods.balanceOf('0xMyWalletAddress').call(); // get the balance of my
wallet address
```

Conclusion

In this article, we've provided a detailed guide on how to interact with the AAVE smart contracts using the Web3 library. We've covered common actions such as lending and borrowing assets, getting the current interest rates, and checking the balance of a contract. With this knowledge, you should be able to write your own Ethereum applications that make use of the AAVE protocol and its various smart contracts.

If you have any questions or need further assistance, you can refer to the AAVE documentation or reach out to the AAVE community for support.

As always, make sure to thoroughly test your code and carefully review the contract terms before interacting with any smart contracts on the Ethereum network. Good luck and happy coding!

Exercises

To review these concepts, we will go through a series of exercises designed to test your understanding and apply what you have learned.

How do you lend 100 DAI using the stable rate model for 1 day using the LendingPool contract in Web3?
How do you borrow 100 DAI using the stable rate model for 1 day using the LendingPool contract in Web3?
How do you get the current interest rate for an asset in the lending pool using the LendingPool contract in Web3?
How do you get the minimum collateralization ratio for an asset in the price oracle using the PriceOracle contract in Web3?
How do you check the balance of a contract or wallet address using the ERC20 contract in Web3?

Solutions

How do you lend 100 DAI using the stable rate model for 1 day using the LendingPool contract in Web3?
To lend 100 DAI using the stable rate model for 1 day using the LendingPool contract in Web3, use the lendStable() method of the LendingPool contract and pass it the contract address for DAI, the amount to lend in wei, and the duration of the loan in seconds. For example:

```
const lendingPool = new web3.eth.Contract(LendingPool_ABI, '0xAAveLendingPoolAddress'); // get the
LendingPool contract
```
```
await lendingPool.methods.lendStable('0xDAIContractAddress', '100000000', '86400').send({ from:
'0xMyWalletAddress' }); // lend 100 DAI for 1 day (86400 seconds)
```

How do you borrow 100 DAI using the stable rate model for 1 day using the LendingPool contract in Web3?
To borrow 100 DAI using the stable rate model for 1 day using the LendingPool contract in Web3, use the borrowStable() method of the LendingPool contract and pass it the contract address for DAI, the amount to borrow in wei, and the duration of the loan in seconds. For example:

```
const lendingPool = new web3.eth.Contract(LendingPool_ABI, '0xAAveLendingPoolAddress'); // get the
LendingPool contract
```
```
await lendingPool.methods.borrowStable('0xDAIContractAddress', '100000000', '86400').send({ from:
```

```
'0xMyWalletAddress' }); // borrow 100 DAI for 1 day (86400 seconds)
```

How do you get the current interest rate for an asset in the lending pool using the LendingPool contract in Web3?

To get the current interest rate for an asset in the lending pool using the LendingPool contract in Web3, use the getCurrentVariableInterestRate() method of the LendingPool contract and call it. This method takes no arguments and returns the current interest rate as a BigNumber object. For example:

```
const lendingPool = new web3.eth.Contract(LendingPool_ABI, '0xAAveLendingPoolAddress'); // get the
LendingPool contract
```

```
const interestRate = await lendingPool.methods.getCurrentVariableInterestRate().call(); // get the
current interest rate for the asset
```

How do you get the minimum collateralization ratio for an asset in the price oracle using the PriceOracle contract in Web3?

To get the minimum collateralization ratio for an asset in the price oracle using the PriceOracle contract in Web3, use the getMinimumCollateralizationRatio() method of the PriceOracle contract and call it. This method takes no arguments and returns the minimum collateralization ratio as a BigNumber object. For example:

```
const priceOracle = new web3.eth.Contract(PriceOracle_ABI, '0xAAvePriceOracleAddress'); // get the
PriceOracle contract
```

```
const                    minCollateralizationRatio                    =                    await
priceOracle.methods.getMinimumCollateralizationRatio().call(); // get the minimum collateralization
ratio for the asset
```

How do you check the balance of a contract or wallet address using the ERC20 contract in Web3?

To check the balance of a contract or wallet address using the ERC20 contract in Web3, use the balanceOf() method of the ERC20 contract and pass it the address you want to check the balance for. This method takes an address as an argument and returns the balance of that address as a BigNumber object. For example:

```
const erc20 = new web3.eth.Contract(ERC20_ABI, '0xEeeeEeeeEeEeeEeEeEeeEEEeeeeEeeeeeeeEEeE'); //
get the ERC20 contract for the asset
```

```
const balance = await erc20.methods.balanceOf('0xMyWalletAddress').call(); // get the balance of my
wallet address
```

UNDERSTANDING THE LENDING AND BORROWING PROCESS ON AAVE

The AAVE protocol is a decentralized platform for lending and borrowing cryptocurrencies. It allows users to earn interest on their idle assets by lending them out to borrowers, and also allows borrowers to obtain short-term loans using their assets as collateral.

In this article, we'll delve into the details of how the lending and borrowing process works on AAVE. We'll cover the different types of loans available, the terms and conditions of each loan, and the key components of the AAVE protocol that facilitate the lending and borrowing process.

Types of Loans

AAVE offers two types of loans: variable rate loans and stable rate loans.

Variable rate loans are loans with interest rates that fluctuate based on the supply and demand of the asset being lent or borrowed. Borrowers and lenders both bear the risk of changing interest rates, which can be both a positive and negative depending on market conditions. However, variable rate loans offer the potential for higher returns on idle assets, as well as lower borrowing costs in times of low demand.

Stable rate loans are loans with fixed interest rates that do not fluctuate based on market conditions. Borrowers and lenders both benefit from the stability of stable rate loans, as there is no risk of sudden changes in interest rates. However, stable rate loans may offer lower returns on idle assets and higher borrowing costs compared to variable rate loans.

Terms and Conditions

The terms and conditions of a loan on AAVE depend on the type of loan and the specific asset being lent or borrowed. Some common terms and conditions include:

- Collateral: AAVE requires borrowers to provide collateral in the form of an asset that is worth more than the value of the loan. The collateralization ratio (i.e., the value of the collateral divided by the value of the loan) must be above the minimum collateralization ratio set by the AAVE protocol for the specific asset. If the collateralization ratio falls below the minimum, the borrower may be required to top up the collateral or the loan may be liquidated to cover the shortfall.
- Interest rate: The interest rate for a loan on AAVE is either fixed or variable, depending

on the type of loan. The interest rate is used to calculate the interest on the loan, which is paid by the borrower to the lender.

- Duration: The duration of a loan on AAVE is the length of time that the loan is active. For variable rate loans, the duration can be as short as a few hours, while for stable rate loans, the minimum duration is usually one day.
- Fees: AAVE charges a small fee for each loan transaction, which is paid by the borrower to the protocol. The fee is used to cover the costs of running the AAVE platform and to incentivize the validators who maintain the platform.

Key Components

The AAVE protocol consists of several key components that facilitate the lending and borrowing process:

- LendingPool: The LendingPool is a smart contract that acts as a central repository for all loans on AAVE. It allows users to lend and borrow assets using either the variable rate model or the stable rate model. The LendingPool also manages the collateralization ratios of borrowers and the distribution of interest payments to lenders.
- PriceOracle: The PriceOracle is a smart contract that provides real-time prices for assets on AAVE. It is used to calculate the value of collateral, the interest rates for loans, and the fees for transactions. The PriceOracle is fed data from multiple external price feeds to ensure the accuracy and reliability of its prices.
- ERC20: The ERC20 is a standard interface for tokens on the Ethereum blockchain. AAVE uses ERC20 tokens as the primary means of lending and borrowing assets on the platform. Users must first wrap their assets in an ERC20 token before they can be added to the LendingPool.
- FlashLoans: FlashLoans are short-term loans that can be taken out and repaid within a single transaction. They are called "flash" loans because they are completed almost instantly, without the need for collateral or a credit check. FlashLoans are useful for executing arbitrage strategies or for testing smart contracts without putting your assets at risk.

Conclusion

In summary, AAVE is a decentralized platform that enables users to earn interest on their idle assets by lending them out, or to obtain short-term loans using their assets as collateral. The AAVE protocol consists of several key components, including the LendingPool, the PriceOracle, and the ERC20 standard, which facilitate the lending and borrowing process. Whether you are a lender looking to earn returns on your idle assets or a borrower in need of short-term financing, AAVE offers a range of options to suit your needs.

Exercises

To review these concepts, we will go through a series of exercises designed to test your understanding and apply what you have learned.

What is the difference between a variable rate loan and a stable rate loan on AAVE?
What is the collateralization ratio and how is it used on AAVE?
What is the role of the PriceOracle in the AAVE protocol?

How do you check the balance of an ERC20 token contract or wallet address using the ERC20 contract in Web3?

How do you take out and repay a flash loan using the AAVE protocol in Web3?

Solutions

What is the difference between a variable rate loan and a stable rate loan on AAVE?

A variable rate loan is a loan with an interest rate that fluctuates based on the supply and demand of the asset being lent or borrowed. Borrowers and lenders both bear the risk of changing interest rates, which can be both a positive and negative depending on market conditions. A stable rate loan is a loan with a fixed interest rate that does not fluctuate based on market conditions. Borrowers and lenders both benefit from the stability of stable rate loans, but they may offer lower returns on idle assets and higher borrowing costs compared to variable rate loans.

What is the collateralization ratio and how is it used on AAVE?

The collateralization ratio is the value of the collateral divided by the value of the loan. On AAVE, borrowers are required to provide collateral in the form of an asset that is worth more than the value of the loan. The collateralization ratio must be above the minimum collateralization ratio set by the AAVE protocol for the specific asset. If the collateralization ratio falls below the minimum, the borrower may be required to top up the collateral or the loan may be liquidated to cover the shortfall.

What is the role of the PriceOracle in the AAVE protocol?

The PriceOracle is a smart contract that provides real-time prices for assets on AAVE. It is used to calculate the value of collateral, the interest rates for loans, and the fees for transactions. The PriceOracle is fed data from multiple external price feeds to ensure the accuracy and reliability of its prices.

How do you check the balance of an ERC20 token contract or wallet address using the ERC20 contract in Web3?

To check the balance of an ERC20 token contract or wallet address using the ERC20 contract in Web3, use the balanceOf() method of the ERC20 contract and pass it the address you want to check the balance for. This method takes an address as an argument and returns the balance of that address as a BigNumber object. For example:

```
const erc20 = new web3.eth.Contract(ERC20_ABI, '0xEeeeeEeeeEeEeeEeEeEeeEEEeeeeEeeeeeeeEEeE'); // get the ERC20 contract for the token

const balance = await erc20.methods.balanceOf('0xMyWalletAddress').call(); // get the balance of my wallet address
```

How do you take out and repay a flash loan using the AAVE protocol in Web3?

To take out and repay a flash loan using the AAVE protocol in Web3, you can use the flashLoan() method of the LendingPool contract and pass it the amount of the loan and the recipient address. This method takes an amount in wei and an address as arguments and returns the flash loan as a transaction object. You can then use the send() method of the transaction object to execute the flash loan and the repayFlashLoan() method of the LendingPool contract to repay the loan. For example:

```
const lendingPool = new web3.eth.Contract(LendingPool_ABI, '0xAAveLendingPoolAddress'); // get the
LendingPool contract
```

```
const flashLoanTx = await lendingPool.methods.flashLoan(100, '0xMyRecipientAddress').send({ from:
'0xMyWalletAddress' }); // take out the flash loan
```

```
await          lendingPool.methods.repayFlashLoan(flashLoanTx.transactionHash).send({          from:
'0xMyWalletAddress' }); // repay the flash loan
```

IMPLEMENTING LENDING AND BORROWING FUNCTIONALITY IN YOUR CODE

Now that you have a solid understanding of the AAVE protocol and its key components, it's time to start implementing lending and borrowing functionality in your code. In this article, we'll cover the steps you need to take to set up a simple lending and borrowing application using AAVE and Web3. We'll walk you through the process of connecting to the AAVE network, interacting with the LendingPool contract, and implementing the core lending and borrowing functionality.

Prerequisites

Before you begin, you'll need to make sure you have the following tools and dependencies installed:

- Node.js: You'll need Node.js installed on your machine to run the code in this article. You can download the latest version of Node.js from the official website.
- npm: npm is the package manager for Node.js. You'll need it to install the dependencies for this project. npm is included with Node.js, so you don't need to install it separately.
- Web3.js: Web3.js is a library for interacting with the Ethereum blockchain. You'll use it to connect to the AAVE network and interact with the AAVE contracts.
- @aave/aave-js: This is the official AAVE library for JavaScript. You'll use it to access the LendingPool contract and other AAVE contracts.

To install these dependencies, create a new directory for your project and run the following commands:

```
npm init
```
```
npm install web3
```
```
npm install @aave/aave-js
```

Connecting to the AAVE Network

To connect to the AAVE network, you'll need an Ethereum wallet that contains some test Ether. You can use MetaMask or another Web3 wallet to create a new wallet and obtain some test Ether from a faucet. Once you have a wallet with test Ether, you can use Web3.js to connect to the AAVE network.

To connect to the AAVE network, you'll need to specify the network URL and the wallet address. The network URL is the endpoint of the Ethereum node that you want to connect to. For the mainnet, the URL is https://mainnet.aave.com. For the testnet, the URL is https://testnet.aave.com.

To connect to the AAVE network, you can use the HttpProvider class from Web3.js and pass it the network URL as an argument. Then, you can use the eth.accounts.wallet.add() method to add your wallet address to the wallet. You can also use the eth.getBalance() method to check the balance of your wallet.

Here's an example of how to connect to the AAVE network and check the balance of your wallet:

```
const Web3 = require('web3');
const networkURL = 'https://testnet.aave.com'; // the URL of the Ethereum node
const walletAddress = '0xMyWalletAddress'; // the address of your wallet
const web3 = new Web3(new Web3.providers.HttpProvider(networkURL)); // create a new Web3 instance
web3.eth.accounts.wallet.add(walletAddress); // add your wallet address to the wallet
const balance = web3.eth.getBalance(walletAddress); // get the balance of your wallet
console.log(balance); // print the balance
```

Interacting with the LendingPool Contract

Now that you're connected to the AAVE network, you can start interacting with the LendingPool contract. The LendingPool contract is the main contract on AAVE that enables users to lend and borrow assets. It contains several methods that you can use to perform lending and borrowing operations.

To interact with the LendingPool contract, you'll need to know the contract address and the ABI (Application Binary Interface). The contract address is the Ethereum address of the LendingPool contract on the AAVE network. The ABI is a JSON object that defines the methods and events of the contract.

To get the contract address and the ABI, you can use the aave.lendingPool.address and aave.lendingPool.abi properties of the aave-js library, respectively. Here's an example of how to get the contract address and the ABI:

```
const Aave = require('@aave/aave-js');
const aave = new Aave(web3); // create a new Aave instance
const lendingPoolAddress = aave.lendingPool.address; // get the contract address
const lendingPoolABI = aave.lendingPool.abi; // get the contract ABI
```

Once you have the contract address and the ABI, you can use the eth.Contract() method from Web3.js to create a contract instance. You can then use the instance to call the methods of the contract.

Here's an example of how to create a contract instance for the LendingPool contract:

```
const lendingPool = new web3.eth.Contract(lendingPoolABI, lendingPoolAddress); // create a contract instance
```

Lending and Borrowing Functionality

Now that you have a contract instance for the LendingPool contract, you can start implementing the core lending and borrowing functionality in your code.

To lend an asset using the AAVE protocol, you can use the lend() method of the LendingPool contract. This method takes an asset address, an amount in wei, and a duration in seconds as arguments, and returns a transaction object. You can then use the send() method of the transaction object to execute the transaction.

Here's an example of how to lend an asset using the AAVE protocol:

```
const assetAddress = '0xMyAssetAddress'; // the address of the asset you want to lend
const amount = 100; // the amount of the asset you want to lend (in wei)
const duration = 86400; // the duration of the loan (in seconds)
const lendTx = await lendingPool.methods.lend(assetAddress, amount, duration).send({ from: walletAddress }); // lend the asset
```

To borrow an asset using the AAVE protocol, you can use the borrow()method of the LendingPool contract. This method takes an asset address, an amount in wei, and a duration in seconds as arguments, and returns a transaction object. You can then use the send() method of the transaction object to execute the transaction.

Here's an example of how to borrow an asset using the AAVE protocol:

```
const assetAddress = '0xMyAssetAddress'; // the address of the asset you want to borrow
const amount = 100; // the amount of the asset you want to borrow (in wei)
const duration = 86400; // the duration of the loan (in seconds)
const borrowTx = await lendingPool.methods.borrow(assetAddress, amount, duration).send({ from: walletAddress }); // borrow the asset
```

Conclusion

In this article, we covered the steps you need to take to set up a simple lending and borrowing application using AAVE and Web3. We showed you how to connect to the AAVE network, interact with the LendingPool contract, and implement the core lending and borrowing functionality in your code. With these tools and techniques, you can start building applications that leverage the power of the AAVE protocol and the Ethereum blockchain.

Exercises

To review these concepts, we will go through a series of exercises designed to test your understanding and apply what you have learned.

Create a function that takes an asset address and an amount in wei as arguments and returns the available supply of the asset on AAVE.

Create a function that takes an asset address and an amount in wei as arguments and returns the maximum amount of the asset that can be borrowed on AAVE.

Create a function that takes an asset address, an amount in wei, and a duration in seconds as

arguments and returns the estimated cost of borrowing the asset on AAVE.

Create a function that takes an asset address and an amount in wei as arguments and returns the total supply of the asset on AAVE.

Create a function that takes an asset address and an amount in wei as arguments and returns the amount of the asset that is currently borrowed on AAVE.

Solutions

Create a function that takes an asset address and an amount in wei as arguments and returns the available supply of the asset on AAVE.

```
async function getAvailableSupply(assetAddress, amount) {
  const availableSupply = await lendingPool.methods.getAssetAvailableSupply(assetAddress).call();
  return availableSupply;
}
```

Create a function that takes an asset address and an amount in wei as arguments and returns the maximum amount of the asset that can be borrowed on AAVE.

```
async function getMaxBorrow(assetAddress, amount) {
  const maxBorrow = await lendingPool.methods.getAssetMaxBorrow(assetAddress).call();
  return maxBorrow;
}
```

Create a function that takes an asset address, an amount in wei, and a duration in seconds as arguments and returns the estimated cost of borrowing the asset on AAVE.

```
async function getBorrowCost(assetAddress, amount, duration) {
  const borrowCost = await lendingPool.methods.getBorrowCost(assetAddress, amount, duration).call();
  return borrowCost;
}
```

Create a function that takes an asset address and an amount in wei as arguments and returns the total supply of the asset on AAVE.

```
async function getTotalSupply(assetAddress, amount) {
  const totalSupply = await lendingPool.methods.getTotalSupply(assetAddress).call();
  return totalSupply;
}
```

Create a function that takes an asset address and an amount in wei as arguments and returns the amount of the asset that is currently borrowed on AAVE.

```
async function getBorrowedAmount(assetAddress, amount) {
  const borrowedAmount = await lendingPool.methods.getBorrowedAmount(assetAddress).call();
  return borrowedAmount;
```

UNDERSTANDING LIQUIDATION AND COLLATERAL IN AAVE

In the AAVE protocol, liquidation and collateral play a crucial role in ensuring the stability of the lending and borrowing market. In this article, we'll take a deep dive into the concepts of liquidation and collateral and how they work in the AAVE protocol.

What is Liquidation?

When a borrower defaults on a loan, the lender is at risk of losing their investment. To protect themselves, lenders can choose to liquidate the borrower's collateral, which is the asset that the borrower put up as security for the loan.

In the AAVE protocol, liquidation is a process that allows lenders to sell a borrower's collateral to recover their investment in case the borrower defaults on the loan. The AAVE protocol has a built-in liquidation mechanism that automatically triggers liquidation when a borrower's loan becomes too risky.

How Does Liquidation Work in AAVE?

The AAVE protocol uses a collateralization ratio to determine when a borrower's loan becomes too risky. The collateralization ratio is calculated as the value of the borrower's collateral divided by the value of the loan. For example, if a borrower has put up 1 ETH as collateral for a 0.5 ETH loan, the collateralization ratio is 2 (1 ETH / 0.5 ETH).

The AAVE protocol has a minimum collateralization ratio that borrowers must maintain to avoid liquidation. If the collateralization ratio falls below the minimum threshold, the AAVE protocol automatically triggers liquidation and sells the borrower's collateral to recover the lender's investment.

The minimum collateralization ratio is set by the AAVE protocol and depends on the riskiness of the asset being borrowed. For example, the minimum collateralization ratio for stablecoins (such as USDC or DAI) is typically lower than the minimum collateralization ratio for more volatile assets (such as ETH or BTC).

What is Collateral?

Collateral is the asset that a borrower puts up as security for a loan. In the AAVE protocol, borrowers can put up a wide variety of assets as collateral, including cryptocurrencies, stablecoins, and even tokenized real-world assets (such as real estate or art).

The value of the collateral is used to determine the size of the loan that the borrower can take out. For example, if a borrower puts up 1 ETH as collateral, they may be able to borrow up to 50% of the value of the collateral, depending on the asset and the loan terms.

Types of Collateral in AAVE

The AAVE protocol supports a wide variety of assets as collateral, including cryptocurrencies, stablecoins, and tokenized real-world assets. Some examples of popular collateral assets on AAVE include:

- Ethereum (ETH)
- Bitcoin (BTC)
- Chainlink (LINK)
- USDC (USDC)
- DAI (DAI)

In addition to these assets, AAVE also supports tokenized real-world assets as collateral. These assets are represented by non-fungible tokens (NFTs) that are backed by real-world assets, such as real estate or art.

Conclusion

In this article, we covered the concepts of liquidation and collateral and how they work in the AAVE protocol. We explained how the AAVE protocol uses liquidation to protect lenders from defaulting borrowers and how collateral is used to determine the size of the loan. We also introduced the different types of collateral that are supported by AAVE, including cryptocurrencies, stablecoins, and tokenized real-world assets. Understanding these concepts is essential for building applications that leverage the power of the AAVE protocol and the Ethereum blockchain.

Exercises

To review these concepts, we will go through a series of exercises designed to test your understanding and apply what you have learned.

Create a function that takes a collateralization ratio and a minimum collateralization ratio as arguments and returns a boolean indicating whether the collateralization ratio is below the minimum threshold.

Create a function that takes a loan amount and a collateral amount as arguments and returns the collateralization ratio.

Create a function that takes a borrower's account address, a loan asset address, and a collateral asset address as arguments and returns the borrower's current collateralization ratio for the loan.

Create a function that takes a borrower's account address, a loan asset address, and a collateral asset address as arguments and returns a boolean indicating whether the borrower's loan is at risk of liquidation.

Create a function that takes a borrower's account address, a loan asset address, and a collateral asset address as arguments and returns the amount of collateral that the borrower needs to add to their loan to meet the minimum collateralization ratio.

Solutions

Create a function that takes a collateralization ratio and a minimum collateralization ratio as arguments and returns a boolean indicating whether the collateralization ratio is below the minimum threshold.

```
function isBelowMinimumThreshold(collateralizationRatio, minimumCollateralizationRatio) {
  return collateralizationRatio < minimumCollateralizationRatio;
}
```

Create a function that takes a loan amount and a collateral amount as arguments and returns the collateralization ratio.

```
function calculateCollateralizationRatio(loanAmount, collateralAmount) {
  return collateralAmount / loanAmount;
}
```

Create a function that takes a borrower's account address, a loan asset address, and a collateral asset address as arguments and returns the borrower's current collateralization ratio for the loan.

```
async function getBorrowerCollateralizationRatio(borrower, loanAsset, collateralAsset) {
  const loanAmount = await lendingPool.methods.getBorrowerLoan(borrower, loanAsset).call();
  const collateralAmount = await lendingPool.methods.getBorrowerCollateral(borrower, collateralAsset).call();
  return calculateCollateralizationRatio(loanAmount, collateralAmount);
}
```

Create a function that takes a borrower's account address, a loan asset address, and a collateral asset address as arguments and returns a boolean indicating whether the borrower's loan is at risk of liquidation.

```
async function isLoanAtRiskOfLiquidation(borrower, loanAsset, collateralAsset) {
  const minimumCollateralizationRatio = await lendingPool.methods.getMinimumCollateralizationRatio(loanAsset).call();
  const collateralizationRatio = await getBorrowerCollateralizationRatio(borrower, loanAsset, collateralAsset);
  return isBelowMinimumThreshold(collateralizationRatio, minimumCollateralizationRatio);
}
```

Create a function that takes a borrower's account address, a loan asset address, and a collateral asset address as arguments and returns the amount of collateral that the borrower needs to add to their loan to meet the minimum collateralization ratio.

```
async function getAmountOfCollateralNeeded(borrower, loanAsset, collateralAsset) {
  const minimumCollateralizationRatio = await lendingPool.methods.getMinimumCollateralizationRatio(loanAsset).call();
```

```
const loanAmount = await lendingPool.methods.getBorrowerLoan(borrower, loanAsset).call();

    const collateralAmount = await lendingPool.methods.getBorrowerCollateral(borrower, collateralAsset).call();

const collateralizationRatio = calculateCollateralizationRatio(loanAmount, collateralAmount);

const difference = minimumCollateralizationRatio - collateralizationRatio;

return difference * loanAmount;

}
```

IMPLEMENTING LIQUIDATION AND COLLATERAL FUNCTIONALITY IN YOUR CODE

In the previous article, we covered the concepts of liquidation and collateral and how they work in the AAVE protocol. In this article, we'll look at how to implement these concepts in your code using the AAVE protocol's smart contracts and libraries.

Prerequisites

Before you begin, make sure that you have completed the following tasks:

- Set up a local AAVE test environment, as described in the "Setting up a local AAVE test environment" article.
- Install the necessary dependencies and tools, as described in the "Installing dependencies and tools" article.
- Familiarize yourself with the AAVE protocol's architecture and key components, as described in the "Overview of the AAVE protocol architecture" article.

Implementing Liquidation

To implement liquidation functionality in your code, you'll need to use the AAVE protocol's LendingPool and LendingPoolCore smart contracts. These contracts provide a variety of methods for interacting with the AAVE protocol and managing loans and collateral.

Here are some examples of common tasks that you can perform using these contracts:

- Check a borrower's current collateralization ratio
- Check whether a borrower's loan is at risk of liquidation
- Calculate the amount of collateral that a borrower needs to add to their loan to meet the minimum collateralization ratio
- Trigger liquidation for a borrower's loan

To interact with these contracts, you can use the aave-js library, which provides a simple, easy-to-use interface for working with the AAVE protocol.

Checking a Borrower's Current Collateralization Ratio

To check a borrower's current collateralization ratio, you can use the getBorrowerCollateralizationRatio() method of the LendingPoolCore contract. This method takes a borrower's account address and a loan asset address as arguments and returns the borrower's current collateralization ratio for the loan.

Here's an example of how to use this method in your code:

```
const Web3 = require('web3');
const { LendingPoolCore, LendingPool } = require('aave-js');
// Connect to the local AAVE test network
const web3 = new Web3(new Web3.providers.HttpProvider('http://localhost:8545'));
// Set the contract addresses
const lendingPoolCoreAddress = '0x24a42fD28C976A61Df5D00D0599C34c4f90748c8';
const lendingPoolAddress = '0x80fB784B7eD66730e8b1DBd9820aFD29931aab03';
// Create instances of the LendingPoolCore and LendingPool contracts
const lendingPoolCore = new LendingPoolCore(web3, lendingPoolCoreAddress);
const lendingPool = new LendingPool(web3, lendingPoolAddress);
async function isLoanAtRiskOfLiquidation(borrower, loanAsset, collateralAsset) {
    return await lendingPoolCore.methods.isLoanAtRiskOfLiquidation(borrower, loanAsset, collateralAsset).call();
}
// Check whether a borrower's loan is at risk of liquidation
const borrower = '0x5E5c5B5f5d5e5F605d6C5b5c5B5f5e5E5f6B5c5D';
const loanAsset = '0x6B175474E89094C44Da98b954EedeAC495481C82';
const collateralAsset = '0xC02aaA39b223FE8D0A0e5C4F27eAD9083C756Cc2';
const isAtRisk = await isLoanAtRiskOfLiquidation(borrower, loanAsset, collateralAsset);
if (isAtRisk) {
  console.log('The borrower\'s loan is at risk of liquidation.');
} else {
  console.log('The borrower\'s loan is not at risk of liquidation.');
}
```

Calculating the Amount of Collateral Needed

To calculate the amount of collateral that a borrower needs to add to their loan to meet the minimum collateralization ratio, you can use the getAmountOfCollateralNeeded() method of the LendingPoolCore contract. This method takes a borrower's account address, a loan asset address, and a collateral asset address as arguments and returns the amount of collateral that the borrower needs to add to their loan.

Here's an example of how to use this method in your code:

```
const Web3 = require('web3');
const { LendingPoolCore, LendingPool } = require('aave-js');
```

```
// Connect to the local AAVE test network
const web3 = new Web3(new Web3.providers.HttpProvider('http://localhost:8545'));
// Set the contract addresses
const lendingPoolCoreAddress = '0x24a42fD28C976A61Df5D00D0599C34c4f90748c8';
const lendingPoolAddress = '0x80fB784B7eD66730e8b1DBd9820aFD29931aab03';
// Create instances of the LendingPoolCore and LendingPool contracts
const lendingPoolCore = new LendingPoolCore(web3, lendingPoolCoreAddress);
const lendingPool = new LendingPool(web3, lendingPoolAddress);
async function getAmountOfCollateralNeeded(borrower, loanAsset, collateralAsset) {
    return await lendingPoolCore.methods.getAmountOfCollateralNeeded(borrower, loanAsset, collateralAsset).call();
}
// Calculate the amount of collateral needed to meet the minimum collateralization ratio
const borrower = '0x5E5c5B5f5d5e5F605d6C5b5c5B5f5e5E5f6B5c5D';
const loanAsset = '0x6B175474E89094C44Da98b954EedeAC495481C82';
const collateralAsset = '0xC02aaA39b223FE8D0A0e5C4F27eAD9083C756Cc2';
const collateralNeeded = await getAmountOfCollateralNeeded(borrower, loanAsset, collateralAsset);
console.log(`The borrower needs to add ${collateralNeeded} ${collateralAsset} as collateral to their loan.`);
```

Triggering Liquidation

To trigger liquidation for a borrower's loan, you can use the liquidateBorrower() method of the LendingPoolCore contract. This method takes a borrower's account address, a loan asset address, and a collateral asset address as arguments and initiates the liquidation process for the borrower's loan.

Before calling this method, you'll need to make sure that the borrower's loan is actually at risk of liquidation. You can use the isLoanAtRiskOfLiquidation() method, as described in the previous section, to check this.

Here's an example of how to use the liquidateBorrower() method in your code:

```
const Web3 = require('web3');
const { LendingPoolCore, LendingPool } = require('aave-js');
// Connect to the local AAVE test network
const web3 = new Web3(new Web3.providers.HttpProvider('http://localhost:8545'));
// Set the contract addresses
const lendingPoolCoreAddress = '0x24a42fD28C976A61Df5D00D0599C34c4f90748c8';
const lendingPoolAddress = '0x80fB784B7eD66730e8b1DBd9820aFD29931aab03';
// Create instances of the LendingPoolCore and LendingPool contracts
const lendingPoolCore = new LendingPoolCore(web3, lendingPoolCoreAddress);
```

```
const lendingPool = new LendingPool(web3, lendingPoolAddress);
async function isLoanAtRiskOfLiquidation(borrower, loanAsset, collateralAsset) {
        return    await    lendingPoolCore.methods.isLoanAtRiskOfLiquidation(borrower,    loanAsset,
collateralAsset).call();
}

async function liquidateBorrower(borrower, loanAsset, collateralAsset) {
        return    await    lendingPoolCore.methods.liquidateBorrower(borrower,    loanAsset,
collateralAsset).send({ from: '0x5E5c5B5f5d5e5F605d6C5b5c5B5f5e5E5f6B5c5D' });
}

// Check whether a borrower's loan is at risk of liquidation
const borrower = '0x5E5c5B5f5d5e5F605d6C5b5c5B5f5e5E5f6B5c5D';
const loanAsset = '0x6B175474E89094C44Da98b954EedeAC495481C82';
const collateralAsset = '0xC02aaA39b223FE8D0A0e5C4F27eAD9083C756Cc2';
const isAtRisk = await isLoanAtRiskOfLiquidation(borrower, loanAsset, collateralAsset);
if (isAtRisk) {
  // Trigger liquidation for the borrower's loan
  await liquidateBorrower(borrower, loanAsset, collateralAsset);
  console.log('The borrower\'s loan has been liquidated.');
} else {
  console.log('The borrower\'s loan is not at risk of liquidation and cannot be liquidated.');
}
```

Note that triggering liquidation is a complex process that involves multiple smart contracts and can take some time to complete. It's also important to note that liquidation is not guaranteed to succeed and may fail if the borrower is able to add enough collateral to their loan before the liquidation process is completed.

To monitor the progress of a liquidation, you can use the LiquidationCallErrored event of the LendingPoolCore contract. This event is emitted when a liquidation call has failed, either because the borrower was able to add enough collateral to their loan or because of an error in the liquidation process.

Here's an example of how to listen for the LiquidationCallErrored event:

```
const Web3 = require('web3');
const { LendingPoolCore, LendingPool } = require('aave-js');
// Connect to the local AAVE test network
const web3 = new Web3(new Web3.providers.HttpProvider('http://localhost:8545'));
// Set the contract addresses
const lendingPoolCoreAddress = '0x24a42fD28C976A61Df5D00D0599C34c4f90748c8';
```

```javascript
const lendingPoolAddress = '0x80fB784B7eD66730e8b1DBd9820aFD29931aab03';
// Create instances of the LendingPoolCore and LendingPool contracts
const lendingPoolCore = new LendingPoolCore(web3, lendingPoolCoreAddress);
const lendingPool = new LendingPool(web3, lendingPoolAddress);
// Listen for the LiquidationCallErrored event
lendingPoolCore.events.LiquidationCallErrored({}, (error, event) => {
  if (error) {
    console.error(error);
  } else {
    console.log(`Liquidation call errored for borrower ${event.returnValues.borrower} on loan asset ${event.returnValues.loanAsset} with collateral asset ${event.returnValues.collateralAsset}.`);
  }
});
```

Selling the Collateral

Once a liquidation is successful, the AAVE protocol will automatically sell the borrower's collateral asset to repay the borrower's loan. The AAVE protocol uses a dynamic auction mechanism to determine the selling price of the collateral asset, which is designed to maximize the recovery value of the loan while minimizing the impact on the market price of the collateral asset.

To monitor the progress of a collateral sale, you can use the LiquidationSucceeded event of the LendingPoolCore contract. This event is emitted when a liquidation is successfully completed and the borrower's collateral has been sold.

Here's an example of how to listen for the LiquidationSucceeded event:

```javascript
const Web3 = require('web3');
const { LendingPoolCore, LendingPool } = require('aave-js');
// Connect to the local AAVE test network
const web3 = new Web3(new Web3.providers.HttpProvider('http://localhost:8545'));
// Set the contract addresses
const lendingPoolCoreAddress = '0x24a42fD28C976A61Df5D00D0599C34c4f90748c8';
const lendingPoolAddress = '0x80fB784B7eD66730e8b1DBd9820aFD29931aab03';
// Create instances of the LendingPoolCore and
const Web3 = require('web3');
const { LendingPoolCore, LendingPool } = require('aave-js');
// Connect to the local AAVE test network
const web3 = new Web3(new Web3.providers.HttpProvider('http://localhost:8545'));
// Set the contract addresses
const lendingPoolCoreAddress = '0x24a42fD28C976A61Df5D00D0599C34c4f90748c8';
```

```javascript
const lendingPoolAddress = '0x80fB784B7eD66730e8b1DBd9820aFD29931aab03';
// Create instances of the LendingPoolCore and LendingPool contracts
const lendingPoolCore = new LendingPoolCore(web3, lendingPoolCoreAddress);
const lendingPool = new LendingPool(web3, lendingPoolAddress);
// Listen for the LiquidationCallErrored event
lendingPoolCore.events.LiquidationCallErrored({}, (error, event) => {
  if (error) {
    console.error(error);
  } else {
    console.log(`Liquidation call errored for borrower ${event.returnValues.borrower} on loan asset ${event.returnValues.loanAsset} with collateral asset ${event.returnValues.collateralAsset}.`);
  }
});
// Listen for the LiquidationSucceeded event
lendingPoolCore.events.LiquidationSucceeded({}, (error, event) => {
  if (error) {
    console.error(error);
  } else {
    console.log(`Liquidation succeeded for borrower ${event.returnValues.borrower} on loan asset ${event.returnValues.loanAsset} with collateral asset ${event.returnValues.collateralAsset}.`);
  }
});
```

Note that the collateral sale is also a complex process that involves multiple smart contracts and can take some time to complete. It's also important to note that the collateral sale is not guaranteed to succeed and may fail if there are errors in the sale process or if the collateral asset is not being sold at a sufficient price.

In the event that the collateral sale fails, the borrower's collateral will be returned to them and the borrower will be required to repay their loan manually. The borrower can then try to add more collateral to their loan and avoid liquidation, or they can try to negotiate a new repayment plan with the AAVE protocol.

Implementing Liquidation and Collateral Functionality in Your Code

Now that you understand the basics of liquidation and collateral in the AAVE protocol, you can start implementing these features in your code.

Here's an example of how you can use the aave-js library to implement lending and borrowing functionality with liquidation and collateral in your code:

```javascript
const Web3 = require('web3');
const { LendingPoolCore, LendingPool, ERC20 } = require('aave-js');
// Connect to the local AAVE test network
const web3 = new Web3(new Web3.providers.HttpProvider('http://localhost:8545'));
// Set the contract addresses
const lendingPoolCoreAddress = '0x24a42fD28C976A61Df5D00D0599C34c4f90748c8';
const lendingPoolAddress = '0x80fB784B7eD66730e8b1DBd9820aFD29931aab03';
// Create instances of the LendingPoolCore and LendingPool contracts
const lendingPoolCore = new LendingPoolCore(web3, lendingPoolCoreAddress);
const lendingPool = new LendingPool(web3, lendingPoolAddress);
// Set the borrower's address and the amount of the loan
const borrower = '0xB7F3989A5b5F3A5e5A5A5eF01DDA48C9d5D543B8';
const loanAmount = '10000000000000000'; // 100 DAI
// Set the loan asset and the collateral asset
const loanAsset = '0x6b175474e89094c44da98b954eedeac495271d0f'; // DAI
const collateralAsset = '0xc02aaa39b223fe8d0a0e5c4f27ead9083c756cc2'; // WETH
// Calculate the amount of collateral needed for the loan
const collateralAmount = await lendingPool.calculateCollateralAmount(loanAmount, loanAsset,
collateralAsset);
// Approve the lendingPool to spend the collateral asset on behalf of the borrower
const collateralERC20 = new ERC20(web3, collateralAsset);
await collateralERC20.approve(lendingPoolAddress, collateralAmount, { from: borrower });
// Borrow the loan asset using the variable rate model and the collateral asset
await lendingPool.borrowVariable(loanAmount, loanAsset, collateralAmount, collateralAsset, { from:
borrower });
// Check the borrower's current collateralization ratio
const collateralizationRatio = await lendingPool.getCollateralizationRatio(borrower, loanAsset,
collateralAsset);
console.log(`Current collateralization ratio: ${collateralizationRatio}`);
// Check if the borrower is below the liquidation threshold
const isBelowLiquidationThreshold = await lendingPoolCore.isBelowLiquidationThreshold(borrower,
loanAsset, collateralAsset);
console.log(`Is below liquidation threshold: ${isBelowLiquidationThreshold}`);
// If the borrower is below the liquidation threshold, trigger liquidation
if (isBelowLiquidationThreshold) {
  await lendingPoolCore.liquidateBorrower(borrower, loanAsset, collateralAsset, { from: borrower });
```

```
}
```

Note that this is just a basic example of how you can implement lending and borrowing functionality with liquidation and collateral in your code. In a real-world application, you may want to add additional error handling and safety measures to prevent errors and ensure that your application is secure and reliable.

Conclusion

In this lesson, we covered the key concepts and functionality of liquidation and collateral in the AAVE protocol. We learned about how the AAVE protocol uses these features to manage risk and ensure that borrowers can always repay their loans. We also saw how to use the aave-js library to interact with the AAVE protocol and implement lending and borrowing functionality with liquidation and collateral in our code.

By understanding these concepts and being able to implement them in your code, you can build more advanced and sophisticated applications on top of the AAVE protocol. You can use these features to build lending platforms, margin trading platforms, and other DeFi applications that require the ability to lend and borrow assets with collateral.

With this knowledge, you are now well-equipped to start building your own applications on top of the AAVE protocol and leverage the power of DeFi to create new financial products and services.

Exercises

To review these concepts, we will go through a series of exercises designed to test your understanding and apply what you have learned.

Write a function that takes a borrower's address and a loan asset as input, and returns the borrower's current collateralization ratio for that loan asset.
Write a function that takes a borrower's address, a loan asset, and a collateral asset as input, and returns the amount of collateral needed for the borrower to reach the liquidation threshold.
Write a function that takes a borrower's address, a loan asset, and a collateral asset as input, and triggers liquidation for the borrower if they are below the liquidation threshold.
Write a function that takes a borrower's address and a loan asset as input, and returns the total amount of fees paid by the borrower for that loan asset.
Write a function that takes a borrower's address and a loan asset as input, and returns the total amount of interest paid by the borrower for that loan asset.

Solutions

Write a function that takes a borrower's address and a loan asset as input, and returns the borrower's current collateralization ratio for that loan asset.
To get a borrower's current collateralization ratio for a particular loan asset, you can use the getCollateralizationRatio() method of the LendingPool contract. Here is an example of how you can implement this function:

```
async function getCollateralizationRatio(borrower, loanAsset) {
```

```
// Create an instance of the LendingPool contract
const lendingPool = new LendingPool(web3, lendingPoolAddress);
// Call the getCollateralizationRatio() method
const collateralizationRatio = await lendingPool.getCollateralizationRatio(borrower, loanAsset);
return collateralizationRatio;
}
```

Write a function that takes a borrower's address, a loan asset, and a collateral asset as input, and returns the amount of collateral needed for the borrower to reach the liquidation threshold.

To calculate the amount of collateral needed for a borrower to reach the liquidation threshold, you can use the calculateAmountToReachLiquidationThreshold() method of the LendingPool contract. Here is an example of how you can implement this function:

```
async function getCollateralNeededForLiquidationThreshold(borrower, loanAsset, collateralAsset) {
// Create an instance of the LendingPool contract
const lendingPool = new LendingPool(web3, lendingPoolAddress);
// Call the calculateAmountToReachLiquidationThreshold() method
const collateralNeeded = await lendingPool.calculateAmountToReachLiquidationThreshold(borrower,
loanAsset, collateralAsset);
return collateralNeeded;
}
```

Write a function that takes a borrower's address, a loan asset, and a collateral asset as input, and triggers liquidation for the borrower if they are below the liquidation threshold.

To trigger liquidation for a borrower if they are below the liquidation threshold, you can use the isBelowLiquidationThreshold() and liquidateBorrower() methods of the LendingPoolCore contract. Here is an example of how you can implement this function:

```
async function triggerLiquidation(borrower, loanAsset, collateralAsset) {
// Create an instance of the LendingPoolCore contract
const lendingPoolCore = new LendingPoolCore(web3, lendingPoolCoreAddress);
// Check if the borrower is below the liquidation threshold
const isBelowLiquidationThreshold = await lendingPoolCore.isBelowLiquidationThreshold(borrower,
loanAsset, collateralAsset);
// If the borrower is below the liquidation threshold, trigger liquidation
if (isBelowLiquidationThreshold) {
await lendingPoolCore.liquidateBorrower(borrower, loanAsset, collateralAsset);
}
}
```

Write a function that takes a borrower's address and a loan asset as input, and returns the total

amount of fees paid by the borrower for that loan asset.

To get the total amount of fees paid by a borrower for a particular loan asset, you can use the getTotalBorrowerFees() method of the LendingPool contract. Here is an example of how you can implement this function:

```
async function getTotalBorrowerFees(borrower, loanAsset) {
  // Create an instance of the LendingPool contract
  const lendingPool = new LendingPool(web3, lendingPoolAddress);
  // Call the getTotalBorrowerFees() method
  const totalFees = await lendingPool.getTotalBorrowerFees(borrower, loanAsset);
  return totalFees;
}
```

Write a function that takes a borrower's address and a loan asset as input, and returns the total amount of interest paid by the borrower for that loan asset.

To get the total amount of interest paid by a borrower for a particular loan asset, you can use the getTotalBorrowerInterest() method of the LendingPool contract. Here is an example of how you can implement this function:

```
async function getTotalBorrowerInterest(borrower, loanAsset) {
  // Create an instance of the LendingPool contract
  const lendingPool = new LendingPool(web3, lendingPoolAddress);
  // Call the getTotalBorrowerInterest() method
  const totalInterest = await lendingPool.getTotalBorrowerInterest(borrower, loanAsset);
  return totalInterest;
}
```

OVERVIEW OF AAVE PROTOCOL GOVERNANCE

The AAVE protocol is a decentralized platform that is governed by its community of users. This means that decisions about the direction and development of the AAVE protocol are made by the community through a transparent and decentralized governance process.

In this lesson, we will provide an overview of the AAVE protocol governance system and how it works. We will cover the key components of the governance system, such as the governance token, the governance forums, and the voting process. We will also discuss the role of the AAVE protocol community in shaping the future of the platform.

What is Governance Token?

The AAVE protocol uses a governance token called "Aave Governance Token" (AAVE) to enable community members to participate in the governance process. AAVE is a standard ERC-20 token on the Ethereum blockchain, and it is used as the primary means of voting on governance proposals.

Holders of AAVE can propose, discuss, and vote on governance proposals through the governance forums. These proposals can range from updates to the AAVE protocol, to the addition of new features or assets, to changes in the protocol's risk parameters.

AAVE tokens can be obtained through various methods, such as participating in liquidity mining programs, buying AAVE on exchanges, or earning AAVE through the AAVE protocol's yield farming and staking mechanisms.

Governance Forums

The AAVE protocol has two main governance forums: the AAVE Governance Dashboard and the AAVE Governance Forum.

The AAVE Governance Dashboard is a web-based platform that allows users to view and participate in the governance process. It is the primary platform for proposing, discussing, and voting on governance proposals. The Governance Dashboard is accessible to anyone with an AAVE token, and it is the main channel for the AAVE community to come together and make decisions about the direction of the protocol.

The AAVE Governance Forum is an online forum for discussing governance-related topics. It is a place for community members to ask questions, share ideas, and engage in discussions about governance proposals and other topics related to the AAVE protocol.

Voting Process

The voting process on the AAVE protocol is based on a stake-weighted voting system, where the voting power of a community member is determined by the amount of AAVE they hold. This means that the more AAVE a user holds, the more influence they have in the voting process.

When a governance proposal is submitted to the AAVE Governance Dashboard, it enters a discussion phase, where the community can discuss and provide feedback on the proposal. After the discussion phase, the proposal enters the voting phase, where AAVE token holders can cast their votes.

Votes are counted using a "time-lock" voting system, where votes are locked in for a certain period of time before the final vote count is determined. This allows for a more accurate and transparent voting process, as it reduces the risk of vote manipulation and ensures that all votes are counted equally.

After the voting period has ended, the proposal is either accepted or rejected based on the outcome of the vote. If the proposal is accepted, it is implemented on the AAVE protocol, and if it is rejected, it is discarded.

Conclusion

In conclusion, the AAVE protocol's governance system is designed to be transparent, decentralized, and community-driven. Through the use of the AAVE governance token, the governance forums, and the stake-weighted voting process, the AAVE community can come together and make decisions about the direction and development of the AAVE protocol.

By participating in the governance process, AAVE token holders have the the ability to shape the future of the AAVE protocol and ensure that it aligns with the needs and interests of the community. Whether you are an experienced developer or a casual user of the AAVE protocol, you can get involved in the governance process and make your voice heard.

Exercises

To review these concepts, we will go through a series of exercises designed to test your understanding and apply what you have learned.

How do you obtain AAVE governance tokens?
What are the two main governance forums for the AAVE protocol?
How is the voting power of a community member determined in the AAVE protocol's governance system?
What is the time-lock voting system and how does it work?
How is the outcome of a governance proposal determined on the AAVE protocol?

Solutions

How do you obtain AAVE governance tokens?
AAVE governance tokens can be obtained through participating in liquidity mining programs, buying AAVE on exchanges, or earning AAVE through the AAVE protocol's yield farming and staking

mechanisms.

What are the two main governance forums for the AAVE protocol?

The two main governance forums for the AAVE protocol are the AAVE Governance Dashboard and the AAVE Governance Forum.

How is the voting power of a community member determined in the AAVE protocol's governance system?

The voting power of a community member in the AAVE protocol's governance system is determined by the amount of AAVE they hold.

What is the time-lock voting system and how does it work?

The time-lock voting system is a method of counting votes in which votes are locked in for a certain period of time before the final vote count is determined. This reduces the risk of vote manipulation and ensures that all votes are counted equally.

How is the outcome of a governance proposal determined on the AAVE protocol?

The outcome of a governance proposal on the AAVE protocol is determined by the result of the vote. If the proposal receives more "yes" votes than "no" votes, it is accepted and implemented on the AAVE protocol. If it receives more "no" votes, it is rejected and discarded.

IMPLEMENTING STAKING FUNCTIONALITY IN YOUR CODE

Staking is a key feature of the AAVE protocol that allows users to earn rewards for providing liquidity and supporting the network. By staking their AAVE tokens, users can earn a share of the fees generated by the AAVE protocol, as well as participate in the governance process and shape the future direction of the platform.

In this lesson, we will cover how to implement staking functionality in your code using the aave-js library. We will go over the different staking methods available on the AAVE protocol and show you how to use them in your code. We will also discuss the key concepts and considerations you need to be aware of when working with staking on the AAVE protocol.

Staking Methods

The AAVE protocol offers several staking methods that allow users to earn rewards in different ways. These methods are:

- Liquidity provision staking: This method allows users to earn rewards for providing liquidity to the AAVE protocol's lending pools. By adding assets to the lending pools, users can earn a share of the fees generated by the loans made from the pools.
- Yield farming staking: This method allows users to earn rewards by providing liquidity to specific yield farming pools on the AAVE protocol. These pools offer higher rewards than the regular lending pools, but they also come with higher risks.
- Staking for governance: This method allows users to earn rewards by staking their AAVE tokens and participating in the governance process. By staking AAVE, users can earn a share of the fees generated by the AAVE protocol and have a say in the direction and development of the platform.

Implementing Staking in Your Code

To implement staking functionality in your code using the aave-js library, you will need to first install the library and set up a Web3 provider. Here is an example of how you can do this:

```
const Web3 = require('web3');
const Aave = require('aave-js');
// Set up Web3 provider
const web3 = new Web3(new Web3.providers.HttpProvider('http://localhost:8545'));
// Set up Aave instance
```

```
const aave = new Aave(web3);
```

Once you have set up the aave-js library and Web3 provider, you can use the staking methods provided by the library to interact with the AAVE protocol.

For example, to stake assets for liquidity provision, you can use the provide() method of the LendingPool contract. Here is an example of how you can implement this method in your code:

```
async function stakeForLiquidityProvision(asset, amount) {
    // Create an instance of the LendingPool contract
    const lendingPool = new LendingPool(web3, lendingPoolAddress);
    // Call the provide() method
    const txReceipt = await lendingPool.provide(asset, amount, { from: userAddress });
    return txReceipt;
}
```

To unstake assets from liquidity provision, you can use the withdraw() method of the LendingPool contract. Here is an example of how you can implement this method in your code:

```
async function unstakeFromLiquidityProvision(asset, amount) {
    // Create an instance of the LendingPool contract
    const lendingPool = new LendingPool(web3, lendingPoolAddress);
    // Call the withdraw() method
    const txReceipt = await lendingPool.withdraw(asset, amount, { from: userAddress });
    return txReceipt;
}
```

To stake assets for yield farming, you can use the provide method of the YieldFarm contract. Here is an example of how you can implement this method in your code:

```
async function stakeForYieldFarming(asset, amount) {
    // Create an instance of the YieldFarm contract
    const yieldFarm = new YieldFarm(web3, yieldFarmAddress);
    // Call the provide() method
    const txReceipt = await yieldFarm.provide(asset, amount, { from: userAddress });
    return txReceipt;
}
```

To unstake assets from yield farming, you can use the withdraw method of the YieldFarm contract. Here is an example of how you can implement this method in your code:

```
async function unstakeFromYieldFarming(asset, amount) {
    // Create an instance of the YieldFarm contract
```

```
const yieldFarm = new YieldFarm(web3, yieldFarmAddress);
// Call the withdraw() method
const txReceipt = await yieldFarm.withdraw(asset, amount, { from: userAddress });
return txReceipt;
}
```

To stake AAVE tokens for governance, you can use the stake method of the AAVE contract. Here is an example of how you can implement this method in your code:

```
async function stakeForGovernance(amount) {
// Create an instance of the AAVE contract
const aaveContract = new AAVE(web3, aaveAddress);
// Call the stake() method
const txReceipt = await aaveContract.stake(amount, { from: userAddress });
return txReceipt;
}
```

To unstake AAVE tokens from governance, you can use the unstakemethod of the AAVE contract. Here is an example of how you can implement this method in your code:

```
async function unstakeFromGovernance(amount) {
// Create an instance of the AAVE contract
const aaveContract = new AAVE(web3, aaveAddress);
// Call the unstake() method
const txReceipt = await aaveContract.unstake(amount, { from: userAddress });
return txReceipt;
}
```

Remember to always call these methods with the correct asset address and amount, and to sign the transaction with a wallet that has sufficient balance and allowance.

With these methods, you can easily implement staking and unstaking functionality in your code for the AAVE protocol.

Additionally, you can use the getStakingData method of the AAVE contract to get information about your staked assets. This method returns an object with the following properties:

- totalStaked: The total amount of staked assets
- stakedBalance: The balance of staked assets
- stakedAllowance: The allowance of staked assets
- totalUnstaked: The total amount of unstaked assets
- unstakedBalance: The balance of unstaked assets
- unstakedAllowance: The allowance of unstaked assets

Here is an example of how you can use this method in your code:

```
async function getStakingData() {
  // Create an instance of the AAVE contract
  const aaveContract = new AAVE(web3, aaveAddress);
  // Call the getStakingData() method
  const stakingData = await aaveContract.getStakingData({ from: userAddress });
  return stakingData;
}
```

You can use this method to get information about your staked assets, such as the total amount of staked assets and the balance of unstaked assets.

With these methods, you can easily implement and interact with staking functionality in the AAVE protocol.

Conclusion

In this article, we learned about the governance features of the AAVE protocol. We covered the different types of staking available in AAVE, including liquidity provision, yield farming, and governance. We also learned how to implement staking and unstaking functionality in our code using the AAVE contract.

With these features and methods, you can easily interact with the AAVE protocol and participate in its governance.

Exercises

To review these concepts, we will go through a series of exercises designed to test your understanding and apply what you have learned.

Write a function that takes in an asset address and amount, and stakes the asset for liquidity provision.
Write a function that takes in an asset address and amount, and unstakes the asset from liquidity provision.
Write a function that takes in an asset address and amount, and stakes the asset for yield farming.
Write a function that takes in an asset address and amount, and unstakes the asset from yield farming.
Write a function that takes in an amount and stakes AAVE tokens for governance.

Solutions

Write a function that takes in an asset address and amount, and stakes the asset for liquidity provision.

```
async function stakeForLiquidityProvision(assetAddress, amount) {
  // Create an instance of the AAVE contract
  const aaveContract = new AAVE(web3, aaveAddress);
```

```
// Call the stake() method
```
```
const txReceipt = await aaveContract.stake(assetAddress, amount, { from: userAddress });
```
```
return txReceipt;
```
```
}
```

Write a function that takes in an asset address and amount, and unstakes the asset from liquidity provision.

```
async function unstakeFromLiquidityProvision(assetAddress, amount) {
```
```
// Create an instance of the AAVE contract
```
```
const aaveContract = new AAVE(web3, aaveAddress);
```
```
// Call the unstake() method
```
```
const txReceipt = await aaveContract.unstake(assetAddress, amount, { from: userAddress });
```
```
return txReceipt;
```
```
}
```

Write a function that takes in an asset address and amount, and stakes the asset for yield farming.

```
async function stakeForYieldFarming(assetAddress, amount) {
```
```
// Create an instance of the AAVE contract
```
```
const aaveContract = new AAVE(web3, aaveAddress);
```
```
// Call the stake() method
```
```
const txReceipt = await aaveContract.stake(assetAddress, amount, { from: userAddress });
```
```
return txReceipt;
```
```
}
```

Write a function that takes in an asset address and amount, and unstakes the asset from yield farming.

```
async function unstakeFromYieldFarming(assetAddress, amount) {
```
```
// Create an instance of the AAVE contract
```
```
const aaveContract = new AAVE(web3, aaveAddress);
```
```
// Call the unstake() method
```
```
const txReceipt = await aaveContract.unstake(assetAddress, amount, { from: userAddress });
```
```
return txReceipt;
```
```
}
```

Write a function that takes in an amount and stakes AAVE tokens for governance.

```
async function stakeForGovernance(amount) {
```
```
// Create an instance of the AAVE contract
```
```
const aaveContract = new AAVE(web3, aaveAddress);
```
```
// Call the stake() method
```

```
  const txReceipt = await aaveContract.stake(amount, { from: userAddress });
  return txReceipt;
}
```

IMPLEMENTING FLASH LOANS IN OUR CODE

Flash loans are a powerful feature of the DeFi ecosystem that allow users to borrow assets without collateral and pay back the loan within the same transaction. This allows users to make arbitrage trades and other complex financial operations that would not be possible with traditional loans.

In this article, we will learn about the flash loan feature of the AAVE protocol and how to implement it in our code. We will cover the different types of flash loans available in AAVE, and how to request, execute, and repay a flash loan.

Types of Flash Loans in AAVE

AAVE offers two types of flash loans: single-asset flash loans and multi-asset flash loans.

Single-asset flash loans allow users to borrow a single asset and repay it within the same transaction. This type of flash loan is useful for arbitrage trades and other simple operations.

Multi-asset flash loans allow users to borrow multiple assets and repay them within the same transaction. This type of flash loan is useful for more complex operations, such as liquidity provision and yield farming.

Requesting a Flash Loan

To request a flash loan, you can use the flashLoan method of the AAVEcontract. This method takes in the following parameters:

- assetAddress: The address of the asset to be borrowed
- amount: The amount of the asset to be borrowed
- recipient: The address of the recipient of the loan (optional)

Here is an example of how you can use this method in your code:

```
async function requestFlashLoan(assetAddress, amount, recipient) {
// Create an instance of the AAVE contract
const aaveContract = new AAVE(web3, aaveAddress);
// Call the flashLoan() method
const txReceipt = await aaveContract.flashLoan(assetAddress, amount, recipient, { from: userAddress });
return txReceipt;
}
```

This method will request a flash loan for the specified asset and amount. If the recipient parameter is provided, the loan will be transferred to the recipient's address.

Executing a Flash Loan

Once a flash loan is requested, it can be executed by calling the executeFlashLoan method of the FlashLoan contract. This method takes in the following parameters:

- assetAddress: The address of the asset to be borrowed
- amount: The amount of the asset to be borrowed
- recipient: The address of the recipient of the loan (optional)

Here is an example of how you can use this method in your code:

```
async function executeFlashLoan(assetAddress, amount, recipient) {
// Create an instance of the FlashLoan contract
const flashLoanContract = new FlashLoan(web3, flashLoanAddress);
// Call the executeFlashLoan() method
const txReceipt = await flashLoanContract.executeFlashLoan(assetAddress, amount, recipient, { from: userAddress });
return txReceipt;
}
```

This method will execute the flash loan and transfer the borrowed asset to the borrower's or recipient's address.

Repaying a Flash Loan

To repay a flash loan, you can use the repayFlashLoan method of the FlashLoan contract. This method takes in the following parameters:

- assetAddress: The address of the asset to be repaid
- amount: The amount of the asset to be repaid

Here is an example of how you can use this method in your code:

```
async function repayFlashLoan(assetAddress, amount) {
// Create an instance of the FlashLoan contract
const flashLoanContract = new FlashLoan(web3, flashLoanAddress);
// Call the repayFlashLoan() method
const txReceipt = await flashLoanContract.repayFlashLoan(assetAddress, amount, { from: userAddress });
return txReceipt;
}
```

This method will repay the flash loan and return the borrowed asset to the lender.

Conclusion

In this article, we learned about the flash loan feature of the AAVE protocol and how to implement it in our code. We covered the different types of flash loans available in AAVE, and how to request, execute, and repay a flash loan. By using these methods, you can easily implement flash loan functionality in your code.

Exercises

To review these concepts, we will go through a series of exercises designed to test your understanding and apply what you have learned.

Write a function that requests a single-asset flash loan for 10 ETH and transfers it to the recipient's address.
Write a function that requests a multi-asset flash loan for 10 ETH and 10 DAI, and transfers them to the recipient's address.
Write a function that executes a flash loan for 10 ETH and 10 DAI, and transfers them to the borrower's address.
Write a function that repays a flash loan for 10 ETH and 10 DAI.
Write a function that executes a flash loan for 10 ETH, transfers it to the borrower's address, and then repays the flash loan.

Solutions

Write a function that requests a single-asset flash loan for 10 ETH and transfers it to the recipient's address.

```
async function requestSingleAssetFlashLoan(recipientAddress) {
// Request a flash loan for 10 ETH and transfer it to the recipient's address
const txReceipt = await requestFlashLoan(ethAddress, 10, recipientAddress);
return txReceipt;
}
```

Write a function that requests a multi-asset flash loan for 10 ETH and 10 DAI, and transfers them to the recipient's address.

```
async function requestMultiAssetFlashLoan(recipientAddress) {
// Request a flash loan for 10 ETH and 10 DAI, and transfer them to the recipient's address
const txReceipt1 = await requestFlashLoan(ethAddress, 10, recipientAddress);
const txReceipt2 = await requestFlashLoan(daiAddress, 10, recipientAddress);
return [txReceipt1, txReceipt2];
}
```

Write a function that executes a flash loan for 10 ETH and 10 DAI, and transfers them to the borrower's address.

```
async function executeMultiAssetFlashLoan() {
```

```
// Execute a flash loan for 10 ETH and 10 DAI, and transfer them to the borrower's address
const txReceipt1 = await executeFlashLoan(ethAddress, 10);
const txReceipt2 = await executeFlashLoan(daiAddress, 10);
return [txReceipt1, txReceipt2];
}
```

Write a function that repays a flash loan for 10 ETH and 10 DAI.

```
async function repayMultiAssetFlashLoan() {
// Repay a flash loan for 10 ETH and 10 DAI
const txReceipt1 = await repayFlashLoan(ethAddress, 10);
const txReceipt2 = await repayFlashLoan(daiAddress, 10);
return [txReceipt1, txReceipt2];
}
```

Write a function that executes a flash loan for 10 ETH, transfers it to the borrower's address, and then repays the flash loan.

```
async function executeAndRepayFlashLoan() {
// Execute a flash loan for 10 ETH and transfer it to the borrower's address
const executeTxReceipt = await executeFlashLoan(ethAddress, 10);
// Repay the flash loan for 10 ETH
const repayTxReceipt = await repayFlashLoan(ethAddress, 10);
return [executeTxReceipt, repayTxReceipt];
}
```

UTILIZING AAVE PROTOCOL FOR STABLECOIN LENDING AND BORROWING

Stablecoins are digital assets that are pegged to a specific asset or currency, such as the US dollar, and are designed to maintain a stable value. They are often used as a means of storing value and facilitating transactions in the cryptocurrency space.

The AAVE protocol, a decentralized finance (DeFi) platform for lending and borrowing, offers a range of stablecoin options for users to lend and borrow. In this article, we will explore how to utilize the AAVE protocol for stablecoin lending and borrowing.

Types of Stablecoins Available on AAVE

AAVE supports a variety of stablecoins, including DAI, USDC, USDT, and TUSD. These stablecoins are pegged to the US dollar and are designed to maintain a stable value relative to the US dollar.

Lending Stablecoins on AAVE

To lend stablecoins on AAVE, you need to first deposit the stablecoins into the AAVE protocol. You can do this using the deposit() method of the LendingPool contract.

```
async function depositStablecoins(amount) {
  // Create an instance of the LendingPool contract
  const lendingPoolContract = new LendingPool(web3, lendingPoolAddress);
  // Deposit the stablecoins into the AAVE protocol
  const txReceipt = await lendingPoolContract.deposit(stablecoinAddress, amount, { from: userAddress });
  return txReceipt;
}
```

Once the stablecoins are deposited, you can lend them to borrowers using the lend() method of the LendingPoolCore contract.

```
async function lendStablecoins(amount) {
  // Create an instance of the LendingPoolCore contract
  const lendingPoolCoreContract = new LendingPoolCore(web3, lendingPoolCoreAddress);
```

```
// Lend the stablecoins to borrowers
    const txReceipt = await lendingPoolCoreContract.lend(stablecoinAddress, amount, { from:
userAddress });
return txReceipt;
}
```

Borrowing Stablecoins on AAVE

To borrow stablecoins on AAVE, you need to first check if you are eligible to borrow by calling the canBorrow() method of the LendingPool contract.

```
async function canBorrowStablecoins() {
// Create an instance of the LendingPool contract
const lendingPoolContract = new LendingPool(web3, lendingPoolAddress);
// Check if the user is eligible to borrow stablecoins
const canBorrow = await lendingPoolContract.canBorrow(stablecoinAddress, userAddress);
return canBorrow;
}
```

If the user is eligible to borrow stablecoins, they can borrow using the borrow() method of the LendingPool contract.

```
async function borrowStablecoins(amount) {
// Create an instance of the LendingPool contract
const lendingPoolContract = new LendingPool(web3, lendingPoolAddress);
// Borrow the stablecoins from the AAVE protocol
    const txReceipt = await lendingPoolContract.borrow(stablecoinAddress, amount, { from:
userAddress });
return txReceipt;
}
```

Repaying Borrowed Stablecoins

To repay borrowed stablecoins, you can use the repay() method of the LendingPool contract.

```
async function repayStablecoins(amount) {
// Create an instance of the LendingPool contract
const lendingPoolContract = new LendingPool(web3, lendingPoolAddress);
// Repay the borrowed stablecoins to the AAVE protocol
const txReceipt = await lendingPoolContract.repay(stablecoinAddress, amount, { from: userAddress });
return txReceipt;
}
```

Using Stablecoins in AAVE Flash Loans

AAVE's flash loans allow users to borrow and repay assets in a single transaction. This can be useful for arbitrage opportunities and other scenarios where assets need to be borrowed and repaid quickly.

To execute a flash loan for stablecoins, you can use the executeFlashLoan() method of the AaveFlashLoan contract.

```
async function executeFlashLoan(borrowerAddress, amount) {
  // Create an instance of the AaveFlashLoan contract
  const flashLoanContract = new AaveFlashLoan(web3, flashLoanAddress);
  // Execute a flash loan for the stablecoins
  const txReceipt = await flashLoanContract.executeFlashLoan(stablecoinAddress, borrowerAddress, amount, { from: userAddress });
  return txReceipt;
}
```

To repay a flash loan for stablecoins, you can use the repayFlashLoan() method of the AaveFlashLoan contract.

```
async function repayFlashLoan(borrowerAddress, amount) {
  // Create an instance of the AaveFlashLoan contract
  const flashLoanContract = new AaveFlashLoan(web3, flashLoanAddress);
  // Repay the flash loan for the stablecoins
  const txReceipt = await flashLoanContract.repayFlashLoan(stablecoinAddress, borrowerAddress, amount, { from: borrowerAddress });
  return txReceipt;
}
```

Conclusion

In this article, we have explored how to utilize the AAVE protocol for stablecoin lending and borrowing. We covered the types of stablecoins available on AAVE, as well as how to lend, borrow, and repay stablecoins using the AAVE protocol. We also looked at how to use stablecoins in AAVE flash loans. By using the AAVE protocol, developers can easily implement stablecoin lending and borrowing functionality in their code.

Exercises

To review these concepts, we will go through a series of exercises designed to test your understanding and apply what you have learned.

Write a function that deposits 1 DAI into the AAVE protocol.
Write a function that checks if a user is eligible to borrow 1 DAI from the AAVE protocol.
Write a function that borrows 1 DAI from the AAVE protocol.
Write a function that checks the current collateralization ratio of a borrower.
Write a function that triggers liquidation of a borrower's position.

Solutions

Write a function that deposits 1 DAI into the AAVE protocol.

```
async function depositDAI() {
  // Create an instance of the LendingPool contract
  const lendingPoolContract = new LendingPool(web3, lendingPoolAddress);
  // Deposit 1 DAI into the AAVE protocol
  const txReceipt = await lendingPoolContract.deposit(daiAddress, 1, { from: userAddress });
  return txReceipt;
}
```

Write a function that checks if a user is eligible to borrow 1 DAI from the AAVE protocol.

```
async function canBorrowDAI() {
  // Create an instance of the LendingPool contract
  const lendingPoolContract = new LendingPool(web3, lendingPoolAddress);
  // Check if the user is eligible to borrow 1 DAI
  const canBorrow = await lendingPoolContract.canBorrow(daiAddress, 1, { from: userAddress });
  return canBorrow;
}
```

Write a function that borrows 1 DAI from the AAVE protocol.

```
async function borrowDAI() {
  // Create an instance of the LendingPool contract
  const lendingPoolContract = new LendingPool(web3, lendingPoolAddress);
  // Borrow 1 DAI from the AAVE protocol
  const txReceipt = await lendingPoolContract.borrow(daiAddress, 1, { from: userAddress });
  return txReceipt;
}
```

Write a function that checks the current collateralization ratio of a borrower.

```
async function checkCollateralizationRatio(borrowerAddress) {
  // Create an instance of the LendingPool contract
  const lendingPoolContract = new LendingPool(web3, lendingPoolAddress);
  // Check the current collateralization ratio of the borrower
  const collateralizationRatio = await lendingPoolContract.getBorrowerCollateralizationRatio(borrowerAddress);
  return collateralizationRatio;
}
```

Write a function that triggers liquidation of a borrower's position.

```
async function triggerLiquidation(borrowerAddress) {
    // Create an instance of the LendingPoolCore contract
    const lendingPoolCoreContract = new LendingPoolCore(web3, lendingPoolCoreAddress);
    // Trigger liquidation of the borrower's position
    const txReceipt = await lendingPoolCoreContract.liquidateBorrow(lendingPoolAddress, borrowerAddress, { from: userAddress });
    return txReceipt;
}
```

INTEGRATING AAVE PROTOCOL WITH OTHER DEFI PROTOCOLS

As a blockchain developer, it is important to understand how to integrate different protocols and platforms to create powerful decentralized finance (DeFi) applications. In this lesson, we will explore how to integrate the AAVE protocol with other popular DeFi protocols such as Compound and Uniswap.

Use Cases for Integrating AAVE and Compound

One potential use case for integrating AAVE and Compound is to create a decentralized lending platform that allows users to borrow and lend a variety of assets. By using AAVE's variable rate model and Compound's algorithmic interest rates, users can take advantage of the best lending and borrowing rates on the market.

Another potential use case is to create a DeFi yield farming platform that allows users to earn returns by staking and lending their assets on AAVE and Compound. By combining the two protocols, users can earn higher returns on their staked assets and have more flexibility in terms of the assets they can earn yields on.

Integrating AAVE and Uniswap

Uniswap is a popular decentralized exchange protocol that allows users to trade a variety of ERC20 tokens. By integrating AAVE and Uniswap, developers can create DeFi applications that allow users to trade and lend assets on a single platform.

For example, a developer could create a DeFi platform that allows users to trade AAVE's aToken assets, which are ERC20 tokens that represent a borrower's debt position on the AAVE protocol. By integrating Uniswap, users can easily buy and sell aTokens on the open market.

Implementing the Integration

To integrate AAVE and Compound, developers can use the aave-js library to interact with the AAVE protocol and the Compound.js library to interact with Compound.

To interact with AAVE, developers will need to first create an instance of the LendingPool contract using the aave-js library.

```
const aave = new Aave(web3);
const lendingPoolAddress = await aave.contracts.getLendingPool();
```

```
const lendingPoolContract = new LendingPool(web3, lendingPoolAddress);
```

To interact with Compound, developers can use the Compound.js library to create an instance of the cEther (Compound Ether) contract, which represents the underlying asset in Compound's lending and borrowing market.

```
const compoundEtherAddress = "0x4ddc2d193948926d02f9b1fe9e1daa0718270ed5";
```
```
const compoundEtherContract = new CompoundEther(web3, compoundEtherAddress);
```

With these contract instances, developers can call functions such as lend(), borrow(), and getBorrowRate() to interact with the AAVE and Compound protocols.

To integrate AAVE and Uniswap, developers can use the Uniswap.js library to interact with the Uniswap protocol and the aave-js library to interact with AAVE.

To interact with Uniswap, developers can use the Uniswap.js library to create an instance of the UniswapExchange contract for a specific token.

```
const uniswapExchangeAddress = "0x5c69bee701ef814a2b6a3edd4b1652cb9cc5aa6f";
```
```
const uniswapExchangeContract = new UniswapExchange(web3, uniswapExchangeAddress);
```

With these contract instances, developers can call functions such as addLiquidity(), removeLiquidity(), and swapExactTokensForTokens() to interact with the AAVE and Uniswap protocols.

For example, to add liquidity to the Uniswap exchange using AAVE's aTokens, a developer could call the addLiquidity() function with the relevant aToken and underlying asset as arguments.

```
const minimumLiquidity = "100000000000000000"; // 0.1 ETH in wei
const deadline = Math.floor(Date.now() / 1000) + 3600; // One hour from now
const aTokenAmount = "1000000000000000000"; // 1 aToken in wei
const assetAmount = "10000000000000000"; // 0.01 ETH in wei
await uniswapExchangeContract.addLiquidity(
  minimumLiquidity,
  deadline,
  aTokenAmount,
  assetAmount,
  {from: userAddress}
);
```

Conclusion

In this lesson, we learned how to integrate AAVE with other DeFi protocols such as Compound and Uniswap. By using the aave-js and Compound.js libraries, developers can easily create powerful DeFi applications that allow users to borrow, lend, trade, and earn returns on a variety of assets.

Exercises

To review these concepts, we will go through a series of exercises designed to test your understanding and apply what you have learned.

Create a decentralized lending platform that allows users to borrow and lend ETH using AAVE's variable rate model and Compound's algorithmic interest rates.

Create a DeFi yield farming platform that allows users to earn returns by staking and lending their assets on AAVE and Compound.

Create a DeFi platform that allows users to trade AAVE's aTokens on Uniswap.

Add liquidity to the Uniswap exchange using AAVE's aTokens and underlying assets.

Write a function that allows the user to borrow an asset from the Compound protocol. The function should take in the following parameters:

– asset: the asset the user wants to borrow (e.g. "DAI")

– amount: the amount of the asset the user wants to borrow

The function should return the transaction hash of the borrow transaction.

Solutions

Create a decentralized lending platform that allows users to borrow and lend ETH using AAVE's variable rate model and Compound's algorithmic interest rates.

To create a decentralized lending platform that allows users to borrow and lend ETH using AAVE's variable rate model and Compound's algorithmic interest rates, you can use the following code as a starting point:

```
// Set up contract instances and web3 provider
const aaveContract = new web3.eth.Contract(aaveAbi, aaveAddress);
const compoundContract = new web3.eth.Contract(compoundAbi, compoundAddress);
const provider = new Web3.providers.HttpProvider(providerUrl);
const web3 = new Web3(provider);
// Set up form for user to enter loan amount and asset
const form = document.getElementById('loan-form');
form.addEventListener('submit', async (event) => {
  event.preventDefault();
  const asset = form.elements.asset.value;
  const amount = form.elements.amount.value;
  try {
    // Borrow asset using AAVE's variable rate model
    const borrowTx = await aaveContract.methods.borrow(asset, amount).send({ from: userAddress });
    console.log(`Borrowed ${amount} ${asset} using AAVE: ${borrowTx.transactionHash}`);
  } catch (error) {
    console.error(error);
```

```javascript
}
});
// Set up form for user to enter lending amount and asset
const lendForm = document.getElementById('lend-form');
lendForm.addEventListener('submit', async (event) => {
  event.preventDefault();
  const asset = lendForm.elements.asset.value;
  const amount = lendForm.elements.amount.value;
  try {
    // Approve asset transfer to Compound
    const approveTx = await compoundContract.methods.approve(compoundAddress, amount).send({ from: userAddress });
    console.log(`Approved asset transfer: ${approveTx.transactionHash}`);
    // Lend asset using Compound's algorithmic interest rates
    const lendTx = await compoundContract.methods.enterMarkets([asset], [amount]).send({ from: userAddress });
    console.log(`Lent ${amount} ${asset} using Compound: ${lendTx.transactionHash}`);
  } catch (error) {
    console.error(error);
  }
});
```

Create a DeFi yield farming platform that allows users to earn returns by staking and lending their assets on AAVE and Compound.

To create a DeFi yield farming platform that allows users to earn returns by staking and lending their assets on AAVE and Compound, you can use the following code as a starting point:

```javascript
// Set up contract instances and web3 provider
const aaveContract = new web3.eth.Contract(aaveAbi, aaveAddress);
const compoundContract = new web3.eth.Contract(compoundAbi, compoundAddress);
const provider = new Web3.providers.HttpProvider(providerUrl);
const web3 = new Web3(provider);
// Set up form for user to enter staking amount and asset
const stakeForm = document.getElementById('stake-form');
stakeForm.addEventListener('submit', async (event) => {
  event.preventDefault();
  const asset = stakeForm.elements.asset.value;
  const amount = stakeForm.elements.amount.value;
```

```
try {
  // Approve asset transfer to AAVE
    const approveTx = await aaveContract.methods.approve(aaveAddress, amount).send({ from: userAddress });
  console.log(`Approved asset transfer: ${approveTx.transactionHash}`);
  // Stake asset on AAVE
  const stakeTx = await aaveContract.methods.stake(asset, amount).send({ from: userAddress });
  console.log(`Staked ${amount} ${asset} on AAVE: ${stakeTx.transactionHash}`);
} catch (error) {
  console.error(error);
}
});
// Set up form for user to enter lending amount and asset
const lendForm = document.getElementById('lend-form');
lendForm.addEventListener('submit', async (event) => {
  event.preventDefault();
  const asset = lendForm.elements.asset.value;
  const amount = lendForm.elements.amount.value;
  try {
    // Approve asset transfer to Compound
      const approveTx = await compoundContract.methods.approve(compoundAddress, amount).send({ from: userAddress });
    console.log(`Approved asset transfer: ${approveTx.transactionHash}`);
    // Lend asset using Compound's algorithmic interest rates
      const lendTx = await compoundContract.methods.enterMarkets([asset], [amount]).send({ from: userAddress });
    console.log(`Lent ${amount} ${asset} using Compound: ${lendTx.transactionHash}`);
  } catch (error) {
    console.error(error);
  }
});
```

Create a DeFi platform that allows users to trade AAVE's aTokens on Uniswap.
To create a DeFi platform that allows users to earn returns by staking AAVE tokens and lending their assets on Compound, you can use the following code as a starting point:

```
// Set up contract instances and web3 provider
const aaveContract = new web3.eth.Contract(aaveAbi, aaveAddress);
```

```javascript
const compoundContract = new web3.eth.Contract(compoundAbi, compoundAddress);
const provider = new Web3.providers.HttpProvider(providerUrl);
const web3 = new Web3(provider);
// Set up form for user to enter staking amount
const stakeForm = document.getElementById('stake-form');
stakeForm.addEventListener('submit', async (event) => {
event.preventDefault();
const amount = stakeForm.elements.amount.value;
try {
  // Approve AAVE token transfer to staking contract
        const approveTx = await aaveContract.methods.approve(stakingContractAddress,
amount).send({ from: userAddress });
  console.log(`Approved AAVE token transfer: ${approveTx.transactionHash}`);
  // Stake AAVE tokens
  const stakeTx = await stakingContract.methods.stake(amount).send({ from: userAddress });
  console.log(`Staked ${amount} AAVE tokens: ${stakeTx.transactionHash}`);
} catch (error) {
  console.error(error);
}
});
// Set up form for user to enter lending amount and asset
const lendForm = document.getElementById('lend-form');
lendForm.addEventListener('submit', async (event) => {
event.preventDefault();
const asset = lendForm.elements.asset.value;
const amount = lendForm.elements.amount.value;
try {
  // Approve asset transfer to Compound
        const approveTx = await compoundContract.methods.approve(compoundAddress,
amount).send({ from: userAddress });
  console.log(`Approved asset transfer: ${approveTx.transactionHash}`);
  // Lend asset using Compound's algorithmic interest rates
    const lendTx = await compoundContract.methods.enterMarkets([asset], [amount]).send({ from:
userAddress });
  console.log(`Lent ${amount} ${asset} using Compound: ${lendTx.transactionHash}`);
} catch (error) {
  console.error(error);
```

```
}

});
```

Add liquidity to the Uniswap exchange using AAVE's aTokens and underlying assets.

To create a DeFi platform that allows users to earn returns by staking and lending their assets on AAVE and Compound and displaying their current balances and interest earned, you can use the following code as a starting point:

```javascript
// Set up contract instances and web3 provider
const aaveContract = new web3.eth.Contract(aaveAbi, aaveAddress);
const compoundContract = new web3.eth.Contract(compoundAbi, compoundAddress);
const provider = new Web3.providers.HttpProvider(providerUrl);
const web3 = new Web3(provider);
// Set up function to display current balances and interest earned
const displayBalances = async () => {
  try {
    // Get current staked AAVE balance
    const stakedAAVE = await aaveContract.methods.balanceOf(userAddress).call();
    // Get current AAVE interest earned
    const aaveInterest = await aaveContract.methods.earned(userAddress).call();
    // Get current Compound balances
    const cTokenBalances = await compoundContract.methods.balances(userAddress).call();
    // Get current Compound interest earned
    const cTokenInterest = await compoundContract.methods.accumulatedInterest(userAddress).call();
    // Display balances and interest earned in DOM
    document.getElementById('staked-aave').innerText = stakedAAVE;
    document.getElementById('aave-interest').innerText = aaveInterest;
    Object.keys(cTokenBalances).forEach((cToken) => {
      const balance = cTokenBalances[cToken];
      const interest = cTokenInterest[cToken];
      document.getElementById(`${cToken.toLowerCase()}-balance`).innerText = balance;
      document.getElementById(`${cToken.toLowerCase()}-interest`).innerText = interest;
    });
  } catch (error) {
    console.error(error);
  }
};
// Set up form for user to enter staking amount and asset
```

```javascript
const stakeForm = document.getElementById('stake-form');
stakeForm.addEventListener('submit', async (event) => {
  event.preventDefault();
  const amount = stakeForm.elements.amount.value;
  try {
    // Approve AAVE token transfer to staking contract
    const approveTx = await aaveContract.methods.approve(stakingContractAddress, amount).send({ from: userAddress });
    console.log(`Approved AAVE token transfer: ${approveTx.transactionHash}`);
    // Stake AAVE tokens
    const stakeTx = await stakingContract.methods.stake(amount).send({ from: userAddress });
    console.log(`Staked ${amount} AAVE tokens: ${stakeTx.transactionHash}`);
    // Display updated balances
    displayBalances();
  } catch (error) {
    console.error(error);
  }
});
// Set up form for user to enter lending amount and asset
const lendForm = document.getElementById('lend-form');
lendForm.addEventListener('submit', async (event) => {
  event.preventDefault();
  const asset = lendForm.elements.asset.value;
  const amount = lendForm.elements.amount.value;
  try {
    // Approve asset transfer to Compound
    const approveTx = await compoundContract.methods.approve(compoundAddress, amount).send({ from: userAddress });
    console.log(`Approved ${asset} transfer to Compound: ${approveTx.transactionHash}`);
    // Get cToken address for chosen asset
    const cTokenAddress = await compoundContract.methods.getCToken(asset).call();
    // Lend asset on Compound
    const lendTx = await compoundContract.methods.supply(cTokenAddress, amount).send({ from: userAddress });
    console.log(`Lent ${amount} ${asset} on Compound: ${lendTx.transactionHash}`);
    // Display updated balances
    displayBalances();
```

```
} catch (error) {
  console.error(error);
}
```

Write a function that allows the user to borrow an asset from the Compound protocol. The function should take in the following parameters:
– asset: the asset the user wants to borrow (e.g. "DAI")
– amount: the amount of the asset the user wants to borrow
The function should return the transaction hash of the borrow transaction.

```
async function borrowFromCompound(asset, amount) {
  try {
    // Get cToken address for chosen asset
    const cTokenAddress = await compoundContract.methods.getCToken(asset).call();
    // Borrow asset from Compound
    const borrowTx = await compoundContract.methods.borrow(cTokenAddress, amount).send({ from: userAddress });
    console.log(`Borrowed ${amount} ${asset} from Compound: ${borrowTx.transactionHash}`);
    // Display updated balances
    displayBalances();
    return borrowTx.transactionHash;
  } catch (error) {
    console.error(error);
  }
}

// Example usage: borrow 100 DAI from Compound
borrowFromCompound("DAI", 100);
```

This function allows the user to borrow an asset from the Compound protocol by taking in the asset and amount as parameters. It gets the cToken address for the chosen asset using the getCToken() method, and then calls the borrow() method of the compound contract to borrow the asset. It then displays the updated balances and returns the transaction hash of the borrow transaction.

RECAP OF KEY CONCEPTS LEARNED IN THE COURSE

In this course, we learned about the AAVE protocol and how to use it as a blockchain developer. We covered a wide range of topics, including the key features and architecture of AAVE, how to install dependencies and set up a local test environment, and how to interact with AAVE smart contracts using Web3.

We also learned about the different types of smart contracts in AAVE, including how to implement lending and borrowing functionality, how to handle liquidation and collateral, and how to utilize AAVE for stablecoin lending and borrowing. Additionally, we explored AAVE governance and how to integrate AAVE with other DeFi protocols.

Below, we will summarize the key concepts learned in this course and provide a recap of the main takeaways.

AAVE Protocol Overview

- AAVE is a decentralized finance (DeFi) protocol that allows users to lend and borrow a variety of assets, including cryptocurrencies and stablecoins.
- AAVE uses a variable interest rate model, which means that the interest rate on loans is determined by the supply and demand for each asset.
- AAVE has a number of key components, including the LendingPool contract, which manages the pool of available assets for lending and borrowing, and the Aave contract, which handles staking and governance.

Installing Dependencies and Tools

- To get started with AAVE development, you will need to install a number of dependencies and tools, including the Truffle framework, Ganache, and the aave-js library.
- You can use Truffle to compile and deploy AAVE smart contracts, and Ganache to run a local blockchain for testing purposes.
- The aave-js library provides an easy-to-use interface for interacting with AAVE smart contracts.

Setting Up a Local AAVE Test Environment

- To set up a local AAVE test environment, you will need to deploy the AAVE contracts to a local blockchain using Truffle.
- You can then use MetaMask to connect to your local blockchain and interact with the AAVE contracts using the aave-js library.

Key Components of the AAVE Protocol

- The LendingPool contract is the main contract for managing the pool of available assets for lending and borrowing. It has a number of methods for lending and borrowing assets, including lendFixed() and borrowFixed() for the fixed rate model, and lendVariable() and borrowVariable() for the variable rate model.
- The Aave contract handles staking and governance in AAVE. It has methods for staking and unstaking AAVE tokens, and for voting on governance proposals.
- The LendingPoolCore contract is responsible for calculating and applying interest rates on loans. It also handles liquidation and collateral management.

Types of Smart Contracts in AAVE

- AAVE has a number of different smart contracts that serve different purposes, including the LendingPool, Aave, and LendingPoolCore contracts.
- The LendingPool and LendingPoolCore contracts are responsible for managing the pool of available assets for lending and borrowing, and for calculating and applying interest rates on loans.
- The Aave contract handles staking and governance in AAVE.

Interacting with AAVE Smart Contracts Using Web3

- To interact with AAVE smart contracts using Web3, you will need to install the web3 library and use it to get the contract instances for the AAVE contracts you want to interact with.
- You can then use the methods of the contract instances to call functions on the contracts, such as lending and borrowing assets, staking and unstaking AAVE tokens, and voting on governance proposals.

Understanding Liquidity

Using liquid in the context of the AAVE protocol refers to an asset that is highly liquid, or easily convertible into cash. This is important because it allows for quick and easy exchange of assets within the AAVE protocol. Lending and borrowing on AAVE relies on the concept of liquid assets, as users must have access to assets that can be easily converted to cash in order to participate in the lending and borrowing process.

In addition to understanding liquid assets, it is also important to understand the concept of collateral within the AAVE protocol. Collateral refers to the assets that are used to secure a loan. In the event that a borrower is unable to make their loan payments, the lender has the right to seize the collateral in order to recoup their losses. It is important to carefully consider the value and liquidity of the collateral being used, as it directly affects the risk of the loan.

Another key concept within the AAVE protocol is governance. AAVE utilizes a decentralized governance model, in which users can participate in the decision-making process by staking their AAVE tokens. Staking allows users to earn returns on their AAVE holdings while also having a say in the direction of the protocol.

Finally, it is important to understand the various types of smart contracts that are used within the AAVE protocol. The AAVE protocol utilizes several different types of smart contracts, including the LendingPool contract and the AAVE contract. These contracts handle important functions such as lending, borrowing, and staking, and it is important for developers to have a thorough understanding of how they operate.

Conclusion

In summary, this course has provided a comprehensive overview of the AAVE protocol, including key concepts such as liquid assets, collateral, governance, and smart contracts. By the end of this course, developers should have a strong understanding of how to utilize the AAVE protocol in their own projects, and be able to implement features such as lending, borrowing, and staking using the aave-js library and Web3.

FURTHER RESOURCES AND TIPS FOR STAYING UP TO DATE

As a developer looking to further your understanding of the AAVE protocol, there are a number of resources available to you.

Further Resources

First and foremost, the AAVE protocol documentation is an excellent resource for understanding the inner workings of the protocol. The documentation covers topics such as the various smart contracts used by AAVE, the protocol's governance model, and the various functions available for developers to utilize.

In addition to the documentation, the AAVE team maintains a number of resources for developers looking to integrate with the protocol. The AAVE GitHub repository contains code examples and libraries that can help developers get started with AAVE, and the AAVE developer portal provides an overview of the different API functions available for integration.

Another great resource for learning about AAVE is the AAVE community forum. Here, developers can ask questions, share their own projects, and engage with other members of the AAVE community. Additionally, the AAVE team often hosts webinars and other educational events, which can be a great way to stay up-to-date on the latest developments in the protocol.

Finally, there are a number of online resources available that provide further information on the AAVE protocol and the larger DeFi ecosystem. Websites such as DeFi Pulse and DeFi Market Cap provide an overview of the DeFi landscape, including the latest trends and top protocols. Additionally, social media platforms such as Twitter and Telegram can be a great way to stay informed on the latest news and developments in the DeFi space.

In conclusion, there are a number of resources available for developers looking to learn more about the AAVE protocol. From the official documentation to online forums and community events, there are plenty of opportunities to deepen your understanding of AAVE and the larger DeFi ecosystem.

Tips for Staying Up to Date

As the DeFi ecosystem continues to evolve at a rapid pace, it can be challenging for developers to stay up-to-date with the latest developments in the AAVE protocol. However, by following a few key tips, you can ensure that you are always in the loop when it comes to new features, updates, and other important developments.

First and foremost, it's important to regularly check the AAVE documentation and other official resources. The AAVE team is constantly working to improve the protocol, and they often release updates and new features that can impact developers. By staying on top of the latest documentation, you can ensure that you are aware of any changes that may affect your integration with AAVE.

Another great way to stay up-to-date with AAVE is to follow the AAVE team on social media platforms such as Twitter and Telegram. The AAVE team is active on these platforms and often shares updates, news, and other important information about the protocol. Additionally, you can join the AAVE community forum, where you can engage with other developers and stay informed on the latest developments in the protocol.

Finally, there are a number of online resources that can help you stay up-to-date with the latest developments in the DeFi ecosystem as a whole. Websites such as DeFi Pulse and DeFi Market Cap provide an overview of the DeFi landscape, including the latest trends and top protocols. By following these resources, you can get a sense of how AAVE is performing relative to other DeFi protocols, and stay informed on the larger DeFi ecosystem.

Conclusion

In conclusion, there are a number of ways to stay up-to-date with AAVE protocol developments. By regularly checking the documentation, following the AAVE team on social media, and keeping an eye on online resources, you can ensure that you are always in the loop when it comes to new features, updates, and other important developments in the AAVE protocol.

THANK YOU

Thank you again for choosing "Learn AAVE DeFi Protocol". I hope it helps you in your journey to learn AAVE DeFi Protocol and achieve your goals. Please take a small portion of your time and share this with your friends and family and write a review for this book. I hope your programming journey does not end here. If you are interested, check out other books that I have or find more coding challenges at: https://codeofcode.org

www.ingramcontent.com/pod-product-compliance
Lightning Source LLC
LaVergne TN
LVHW081801050326
832903LV00027B/2044